KEYS TO BITCOIN

KEYS TO BITCOIN

LEARN HOW BITCOIN REALLY WORKS

Raphaël Meyer, PhD

ISBN: 978-1-7347733-2-3

This book is dedicated to my heroes, Sasha and Zoé.

Table of Contents

Introduction

Why another book about Bitcoin?

Most books written about Bitcoin describe how cryptocurrencies work in broad brushstrokes, while giving you a long list of the "best" coins (of the moment) and throwing in some quick investment advice for good measure. A lot of these books also try to recruit you into the cult of Bitcoin or, on the contrary, to scare you away from cryptocurrencies.

This book focuses on explaining in simple terms the technology behind Bitcoin (and many other cryptocurrencies), but without distorting the key concepts it relies on and without taking a partisan stance. Cryptocurrencies can seem inherently complex because they combine elements of mathematics, economics, and social sciences. They can be explained in simple terms, but the depth of their underlying mechanisms should not be erased completely.

If you buy a car thinking all it needs is gas, you might be unpleasantly surprised when the oil runs out and your engine breaks down. And while cars have all sorts of dashboard indicators to prevent that, cryptocurrencies do not.

Bitcoin is a good starting point to understand cryptocurrencies because it's the original one and, as a result, one of the simplest. It's a fascinating technology. You do not need a degree in math or engineering to understand Bitcoin; all you need is a curious mind.

The book works as follows: First, I will give you a rough understanding of what Bitcoin is, how it compares to other forms of money, and the main actors of its system and their roles. In the following chapters, you will learn basic concepts about cryptography, since that is what all cryptocurrencies are based on. Then you will see what Bitcoin mining really means, how and where bitcoins are stored, and how payments work. Finally, you will discover how Bitcoin has changed so far and how it can continue to evolve to overcome its challenges and limitations.

Chapter 1

Money: From Stone Discs To Bitcoin

1.1 The Stone Money Of Yap

About 800 miles east off the Philippines and roughly the same distance north of Papua (Indonesia) lies the small island of Yap, one of the four members of the Federated States of Micronesia. The island itself is a dozen miles long and a couple of miles wide, and its closest neighbor is Palau, around 250 miles to the southwest, while the US territory of Guam is twice as far in the opposite direction.

It is believed that the first settlers came to this island more than 4,000 years ago. Still, Yap stayed undiscovered by the Europeans explorers until the sixteenth century, and mostly without any significant external cultural influence until the nineteenth century.

While Yap enjoys the seclusion of many islands in this part of the world, what makes it utterly unique is its traditional use of large doughnut-shaped discs of stone as a form of currency. These discs, called *Rai stones*, vary in size and value, the largest ones being about 140 inches wide and weighing more than 8,000 pounds. The stone discs are an ancestral tradition but are still in use today for special occasions such as weddings or land transfers. They usually have high monetary values, the value of a particular stone being proportional to its size and to the difficulty encountered in carving it and importing it to the island. Most stones were quarried in Palau, an island five days away by canoe. These stones are astonishingly beautiful, and their aesthetic quality also contributes to their value. (For more details, google "yap stone money.")

When a village wants to buy some land from another village, for instance, the buyers can give a Rai stone to the sellers for payment. The selling village can later use the stone to buy a different piece of land or trade it for services, such as construction. However, the stone itself, which is usually placed in a public area of the island, does not move. Instead, the people of Yap rely on oral tradition to record the transfer of ownership. Everyone on the small island will quickly hear about which stone has been transferred to whom.

Obviously, not every transaction can be settled in Rai stones, and the people of Yap use other traditional currencies for different occasions, including cloth, shells, and balls of turmeric, as well as the US dollar for everyday purchases. The money supply (in Rai stones) is fixed, as no stones have been imported to the island since the early twentieth century. Modern transportation would have made the importation too easy, and therefore the new stones would have been of much lesser value than the old ones. Value is tied to difficulty.

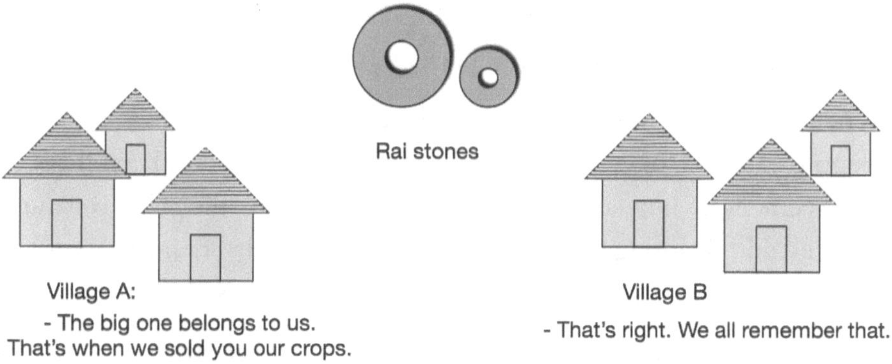

Figure 1 A transaction recorded on Yap island. The Rai stones are used as a support for collective memory.

For all its beauty and simplicity, the stone money of Yap suffers a major drawback: it cannot scale up. The system works for the small population of the island as long as it's used infrequently to record significant transactions. However, it cannot record daily transactions, nor can it be used in a larger area because it relies on the collective memory of the people.

The inhabitants of Yap can undoubtedly remember when a specific piece of land has changed hands and the associated stone's immobile transfer every few years. Still, they would be quickly overwhelmed if they had to remember such transactions for daily expenses, or deal with a much larger population!

So what do people on Yap use for the daily expenses? The mighty US dollar!

1.2 The Green Ink Of The US Dollar

During the American Civil War, Abraham Lincoln asked for demand notes (paper money printed by the government of the Union) to finance the war effort. The bills were printed with green ink on their back to avoid easy counterfeiting and earned the name “greenbacks.” (In contrast, the Confederate bills usually had blank backs.)

When the size of dollar bills was reduced to its modern format in 1929, the supply of green ink was still plentiful so it was decided to keep that color for convenience, but also because—according to the US Bureau of Engraving and Printing—“green was psychologically identified with the strong and stable credit of the Government.” Green was the color of trust.

This story identifies a crucial point, which would be true for any other national currency: the backbone of a national currency is the confidence in the government issuing it. In other words, the US dollar’s value is tied to the general health of the US economy and to the confidence in its government to sustain this economy.

The US is one of the most powerful countries in the world, and its currency is the most used in global exchanges. That is precisely why the people of Yap use the dollar in their daily expenses: there is widespread confidence that the United States will remain a powerful country. Moreover, the dollar is already accepted in so many places around the world.

However, with the cultural and financial influence of China rising on the world stage, this dominance might not last forever. Time will tell whether the future inhabitants of Yap will still pay for their food in dollars, or if they will swap for the Chinese renminbi (or yuan) at some point.

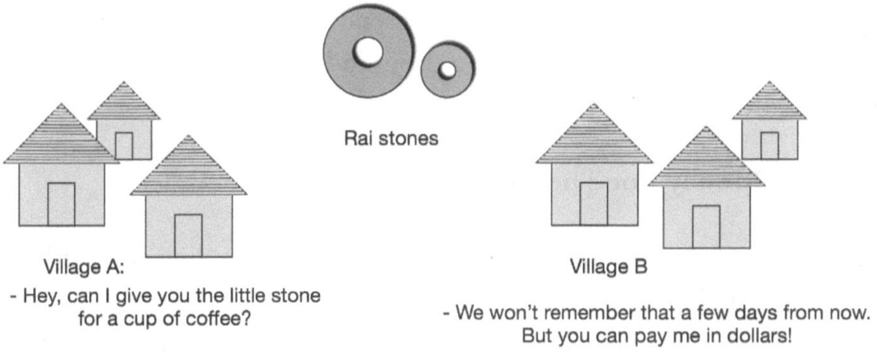

Figure 2 A daily transaction on Yap island. The US dollar is a better tool for that.

In countries where the government is notoriously corrupt and cannot be trusted by its citizens, there is usually little confidence in the official currency, so much so that a parallel economy based on a different currency may appear. An example of this is 2016 Venezuela, where the problems of corruption, high inflation, and general distrust in the government undermined the value of the bolivar, the national currency, and promoted a black market economy of US dollars. Interestingly, two years later in 2018, the confidence in the bolivar had sunken so low that the president of Venezuela was promoting a new national cryptocurrency, the petro, instead.

Let's examine the differences between a national currency like the US dollar and the Rai stones of Yap. The first essential difference is in the supply of money. Whereas there is a fixed number of Rai stones on the island, the dollar supply is not fixed but is controlled by the Federal Reserve's policies: the Fed has the power to print money to increase supply, or to raise interest rates to tighten it.

A second essential difference lies in the way transactions are recorded. Transactions in dollars can occur in bills or through checks and credit cards, but they are mostly private. In contrast, transactions involving Rai stones are public by design: they rely on collective memory.

And finally, another important difference lies in the dollar's inherent capability to scale: whether used by a thousand people or a billion, the dollar works exactly the same.

1.3 Digital Money For The Internet Age

The idea of putting computers in a network and enabling easy and secure exchanges of information dates mostly to the 1960s and was encouraged by the threats of the Cold War (the US military relied exclusively on the telephone at the time). A network of computers communicating between different places, first across the US, then across the planet, started to grow during the 1970s and 1980s; however, it was almost exclusively the domain of research institutions and the military.

Yet in 1989, a computer programmer working at the CERN (the European Organization for Nuclear Research) in Switzerland suggested a different way to see the network: instead of having only one-to-one communications between computers, the network could be used to display information that could be read by everyone. This change in perspective allowed the network to grow exponentially during the next few years and to become the worldwide, pervasive, gigantic grid that we now know as the internet.

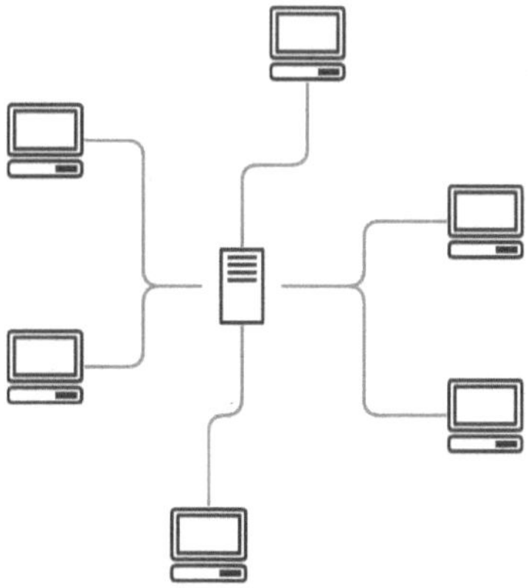

Figure 3 Surfing the web: many users being served the same information (a website) by a central "server."

In the 1990s, internet connections were still painfully slow (and always started with funny sounds), but the invention of new compression techniques allowed users to begin exchanging movies and music files more efficiently. However, if you weren't connected to the internet back then, how would you know where to find a copy of the latest Britney Spears song?

The first large-scale peer-to-peer service, Napster, was launched in 1999. It was a network that anyone with an internet connection could join and where resources (in this case, the users' music collections) were shared by all participants. In other words, everything for everybody for free! Started by two teenagers, Napster became hugely popular very quickly: it attracted more than 20 million users in less than a year. However, within five years, commercial competitors such as Apple's iTunes Store killed the file-sharing craze and drove Napster to near oblivion.

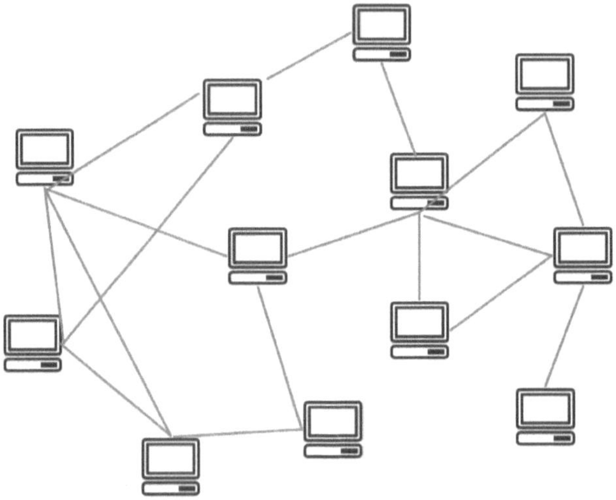

Figure 4 A peer-to-peer network: each user shares some data with a few of its peers, without much structure.

Through the 1990s and 2000s, researchers and software developers started to look for ways to use the model provided by the internet and peer-to-peer networks to create digital currencies. The search was on for money that could be sent as easily as emails but would circumvent the governments and the central banks, just like the peer-to-peer networks ignored borders (and laws). But this was not an easy task: duplicating a $5 bill perfectly might be extremely difficult, but copying a digital file can be done by anyone.

If you have a $5 bill in your wallet and use it to buy a coffee and a newspaper, then you don't physically have this bill anymore; it's in someone else's pocket. But if you have a digital coin and spend it to buy a digital newspaper, you could still keep a copy of that coin on your laptop or on your phone. What would prevent you from spending it again and again? This "double-spending problem," as it is known, was at the heart of the matter.

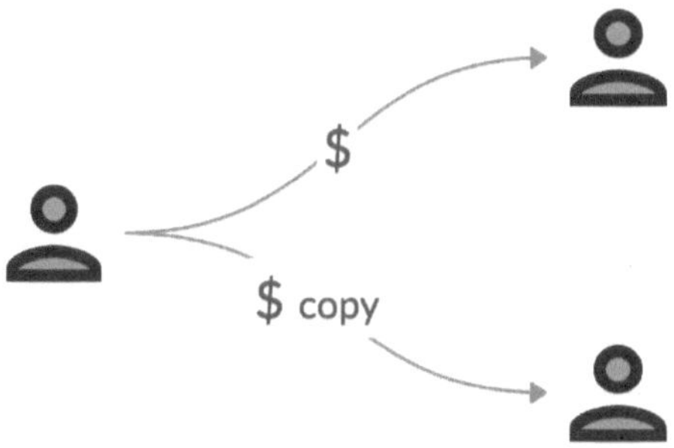

Figure 5 The double-spending problem: digital objects can be duplicated at no cost!

1.4 Bitcoin And The Blockchain

In 2008, a solution to the double-spending problem was proposed by a person (or a group of people) using the pseudonym Satoshi Nakamoto. Satoshi's idea was to record the history of every digital coin and put this history in a ledger that would be accessible to everyone. By making these accounting records publicly available to all, every participant would be able to check that coins were not being spent twice. This new digital money was called Bitcoin.

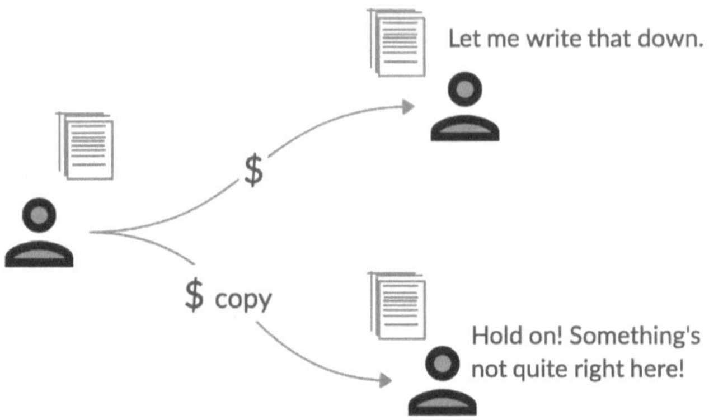

Figure 6 Trying to double-spend with a shared ledger: the second transaction is not valid!

In Bitcoin, participants are not required to act honestly, but they are incentivized to do so. The transactions—the payments—are bundled together into **blocks**, and on average a new block is added to the ledger every 10 minutes. The public ledger later became known as the **blockchain**, the chain of blocks.

The **miners** are the participants who check against double-spending and add new blocks of transactions to the ledger. Similar to miners of the California gold rush, digital miners are rewarded for their efforts: with each block added, a reward (in bitcoins) goes to the miner who "found" it.

To decide who gets to add the latest transactions, Bitcoin puts the miners in competition with each other. They spend electricity and computing time trying to solve a mathematical puzzle called **proof of work**. The miner who finds a solution first gets to add their block to the ledger and receives the reward. Then everyone starts working on the next block of transactions, and so on.

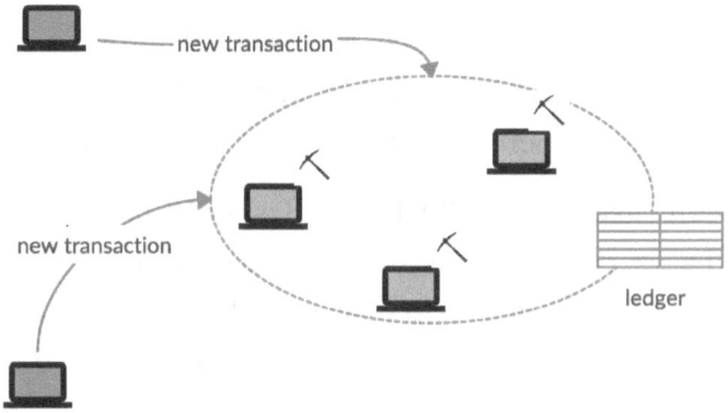

Figure 7 Bitcoin users send new transactions (payments) to the network, while miners bundle the transactions into blocks. The first miner to solve the current proof-of-work puzzle gets the block reward and adds their own block to the ledger.

To discourage tampering, blocks of transactions are timestamped[1] and linked to one another using mathematical properties. Anyone attempting to modify the data of any block will be forced to redo the proof of pork for all the blocks that have been added since. Since solving proof-of-work puzzles takes time and consumes energy, it may be more profitable to be honest: the energy spent tampering with transactions is more advantageously spent keeping the blockchain secure and getting paid for it!

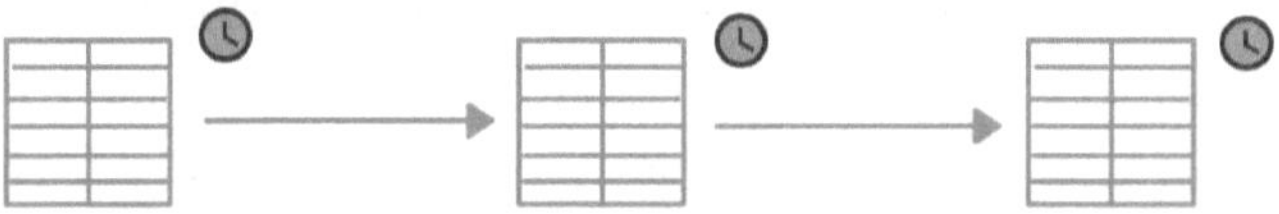

Figure 8 Each block adds a new page to the blockchain. Blocks are timestamped so that the order of the pages is undisputable.

[1] Each block includes a date and time.

The blockchain contains every payment that ever occurred, and anyone can access it.[2] To balance this public exposure of transactions, identities in Bitcoin are not associated with names, as bank accounts are; instead, Bitcoin uses long strings of numbers and letters called **addresses**.

Addresses are like digital PO boxes. Using random-looking addresses grants some degree of anonymity to transactions done in bitcoins, but only to the extent that there is no obvious relationship between a Bitcoin address and its owner. Bitcoin is said to be **pseudonymous** rather than anonymous.

FROM	AMOUNT	TO
1YZeaCpdGF...	12.0577 BTC	12c6DSiU4...
1N5rAhc65y...	0.00034 BTC	bc1qc5e0mkje...
3JN6v7th8NT...	50.9032 BTC	1AK4LYE6PY...
...	...	...
...	...	...

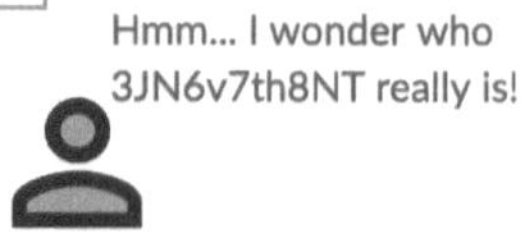

Figure 9 Here are some pseudonymous transactions being recorded in the Bitcoin ledger.

Each transaction specifies that some coins belonging to a particular address are being transferred to another address, just like you would take coins out of your wallet to pay for a coffee. With cash, if you don't have the exact amount, you give a little more and get the change back. Bitcoin works somewhat similarly: you use whatever coins you have in your wallet and get the change back, minus a small transaction fee.

[2] Google "blockchain explorer" and you can read every transaction of every block yourself.

The higher the fee you are willing to pay, the quicker your transaction will be recorded in the blockchain, and thus your payment validated. Transaction fees create a secondary incentive for miners on top of the block reward.

Bitcoin relies on **cryptography**—the area of mathematics that studies encoding and decoding of messages—to make all its parts work together. Hence the name: **cryptocurrency**.

1.5 The Blockchain Is A Digital Collective Memory

Bitcoin can, in theory, be used similarly for daily transactions (like buying a cup of coffee)[3] and for notable ones (like buying a property). In practice, as you'll see later, it is more suited for larger and infrequent transactions, even though that may change in the next few years as newer layers are built on top of the Bitcoin network. We'll come back to that in Chapter 9.

Bitcoin's use is not limited geographically: users can transact from anywhere on the planet as long as they have an internet connection (even an intermittent one).

Yet Bitcoin does not depend on any government or central bank. Instead, its users rely on cryptographic tools and protocols. Users do not need to trust (or even know) each other to transact securely. A consensus about transactions is achieved without mutual trust.

Bitcoin attains this decentralized consensus by using principles similar to the ones used in Yap: if a village of the island tried to cheat, for example by pretending that a particular stone belonged to its inhabitants, even though common public history remembered a different narrative, all the other villages would agree to reject this fraudulent claim and discredit the cheaters.

---

[3] Bitcoin is not the most efficient cryptocurrency for such transactions.

The blockchain is a sophisticated digital and cryptographic evolution of the oral tradition used by the people of Yap: it is a digital collective memory. The difference lies in the medium (digital data vs. stone monuments) and the protocol (cryptography vs. collective memory). These digital technologies allow Bitcoin to extend geographically and to scale up (to some extent, as I'll discuss later). The Rai stones could only work on a small island like Yap, while Bitcoin already has millions of users spread around the world.

Also, remember that each Rai stone receives a value proportional to the difficulty encountered in its carving and shipping. Similarly, bitcoins are created by the miners who solve a difficult mathematical problem. Making the creation of currency difficult is a protection against fraud. Of course, this idea is also at play with the American dollar: the exact color of the ink and more sophisticated features (such as textures and patterns only visible under UV light) prevent the easy counterfeiting of bills.

Finally, the Rai stones of Yap come in limited supply by law: importing new stones came to a halt at the beginning of the twentieth century. The dollar, on the contrary, can be printed at will by the Federal Reserve (as has happened from 2008 to 2013 with the different phases of quantitative easing[4] to sustain the economy, and again in 2019 and 2020).

Bitcoin, unlike the US dollar, has a capped supply. The supply comes exclusively from block rewards, and the "monetary" policy is known in advance: the block rewards are cut in half about every four years. This way, the extra supply of bitcoins added yearly diminishes over time.

---

[4] Quantitative easing is a monetary policy used to quickly increase the supply of money when interest rates are already low. For example, the Fed can buy government bonds, making their price go up and their yield go down. As a result, other assets, such as shares and corporate bonds, look more attractive and investors start readjusting their portfolios, creating more liquidity and making it cheaper for businesses to borrow money.

The decreasing yearly supply is expected to be null around 2140.[5] The total supply will then reach 21 million bitcoins (from about 18.5 million in 2020). This capped supply, independent of any government, creates a very different economy than the one based on the dollar: Bitcoin is closer to a deflationary commodity such as gold than to national currencies.

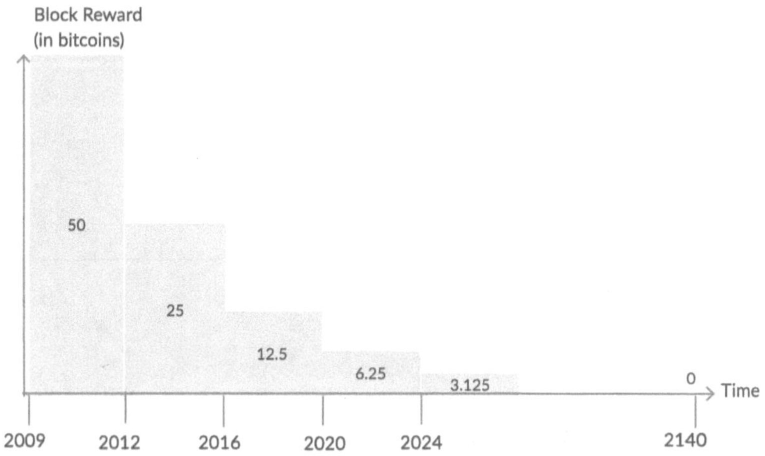

Figure 10 The block reward decreasing exponentially over time.

[5] The year 2140 is an estimation based on roughly four years between each new cut of Bitcoin's supply rate. In reality, changes in the total computing power dedicated to mining can shift the date of this cut by a few months each time.

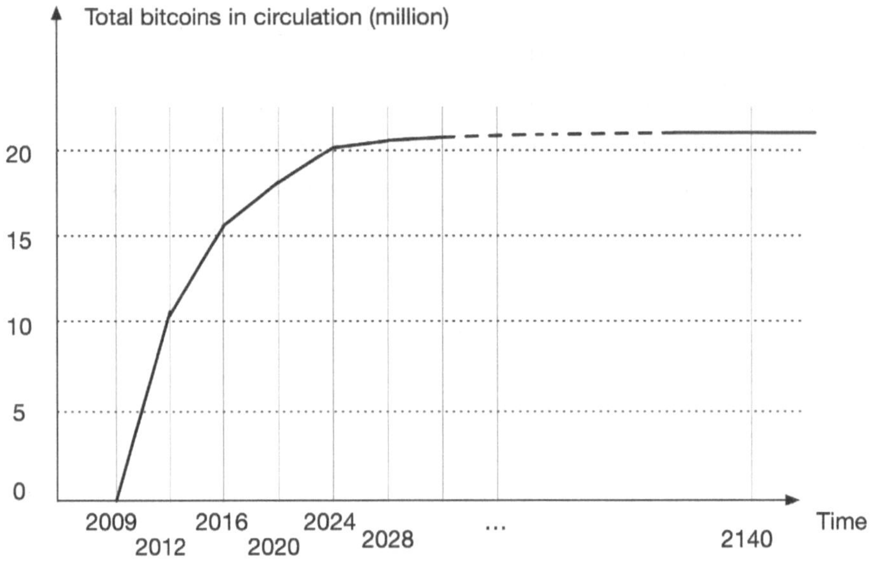

Figure 11 The total bitcoin supply approaching 21 million over time.

1.6 Full Nodes: The Volunteers Of Bitcoin

While new transactions can only be added to the blockchain by miners, who spend computing time and electricity necessary for proof of work, most computers in the Bitcoin network are not miners. These computers, called **full nodes**, play a crucial role: they verify the work of the miners.

Full nodes check that every new block added to the blockchain is made up of transactions that are compatible with the rules of the Bitcoin protocol: in particular, nodes verify that transactions do not create any double-spending. This verification process is called **validation**.

Unlike solving proof-of-work puzzles, validating transactions does not require much computing power. Therefore, many people choose to voluntarily run a full node software program on their computer. Validation can be done even by the smallest of computers, such as the Raspberry Pi, a mobile phone-sized computer that costs less than $100.

Full nodes, which are run voluntarily (there is no financial reward for running a node), provide checks and balances for the network. Even if all the miners decided to band together and make or accept fraudulent transactions, the full nodes would reject their blocks. Bitcoin miners can sometimes sound all powerful, but they are only one part of a system and cannot function alone.

1.7 How It All Comes Together

This first chapter is packed with new concepts and information, and not all of it fits perfectly together. Bitcoin is very different from everything you already know, unless you are familiar with computer science, cryptography, and also economics!

Fear not! This chapter is only meant to give you a rough idea of how things work.

- Users can send each other payments called *transactions*
- These transactions are put together in different pages on a ledger (the blockchain) by miners
- Miners need to spend time and electricity before they can be chosen to write a new page (a block) into the blockchain
- This spending of resources is what keeps the network safe

In the following chapters, you will learn what makes the different parts of the system work together. Let's start by understanding the foundation of all cryptocurrencies: cryptography.

Chapter 2

The Cryptographic Toolbox

As explained in the first chapter, cryptocurrencies replace trusting governments with trusting a decentralized protocol based on mathematical properties. To see how this is possible, let's start with a brief history of cryptography.

2.1 Caesar's Wars

Cryptography, the art and science of keeping secrets, has been around for at least the last four millennia, and probably since humans started to organize in clans and tribes.

In the first century CE, Julius Caesar was already using basic cryptographic methods to encrypt messages sent to his generals. The cipher (encoding method) he used was simple: he considered each letter of the message and shifted it up three places in the alphabet, so A became D, B became E, and so on. Toward the end of the alphabet, the letters wrapped around to the beginning of the alphabet so that X became A, Y became B, and Z became C. (See Figure 12.)

A	B	C	D	E	F	G	H	...	...	...
D	E	F	G	H	I	J	K	...	...	...

Figure 12 Principle of encoding with Caesar's cipher. To decode, simply reverse the arrow.

For example, the message "VENI VIDI VICI"[6] would be encrypted as "YHQL YLGL YLFL."

To decrypt a message, his generals would simply reverse the process by shifting each letter down three places in the alphabet. For example, if they received a message that read "DOHD LDFWD HVW," they could use the decoding table of Figure 13 to decrypt the message, where each letter with a grey background is replaced by the letter below it with the white background. Can you decipher the message using Figure 13?[7]

A	B	C	D	E	F	G	H	I	J	K	L	M
X	Y	Z	A	B	C	D	E	F	G	H	I	J

N	O	P	Q	R	S	T	U	V	W	X	Y	Z
K	L	M	N	O	P	Q	R	S	T	U	V	W

Figure 13 Decoding table: Replace each letter with a grey background with the corresponding one with the white background.

Such an encryption technique was rudimentary: the secrecy of the messages relied entirely on the encryption protocol itself remaining secret. You can use different Caesar ciphers by changing the number of shifts applied to letters. However, once the protocol is known, it is not hard for an

---

[6] Translated from Latin, this means "I came, I saw, I conquered."
[7] The answer is the Latin phrase "ALEA IACTA EST," or in English, "The die is cast."

enemy to guess which variant of the cipher was used: just try all 26 variants and see which ones yield decrypted messages that make sense.

While this attempt at keeping secrets was clever and must have worked for a while, certainly one day the secret protocol fell into the enemy's ear and it became useless. Surprisingly, variants of this simple cipher were still used quite recently: Italian mafia boss Bernardo Provenzano, who was arrested in 2006, used this method to conceal names in messages written to his lieutenants.

2.2 The Vigenère Cipher

During the sixteenth century, the idea of Caesar's encryption protocol was improved by several people, and the result would become later known as the *Vigenère cipher*. Instead of always shifting the letters of the original message by a fixed number (three in the case of Caesar's cipher), one would use a secret word called a **key**, and shift the first letter of the message by the same number of places as the position of the first letter of the key, and so on.

For example, if the key was "FISH," the first letter of the original message would be shifted by six places (because F is the sixth letter of the alphabet), the second letter of the message would be shifted by nine places (because I is the ninth letter of the alphabet), then the next letter would be shifted by nineteen positions (for S), the next one by eight places (for H), then they would keep going using F, I, S, H.

This can also be done using a Vigenère table, where each row corresponds to an increased shift of the alphabet. (See Figure 14.)

	A	B	C	D	E	F	G	H	I	J	K	L	…
A	B	C	D	E	F	G	H	I	J	K	L	M	…
B	C	D	E	F	G	H	I	J	K	L	M	N	…
C	D	E	F	G	H	I	J	K	L	M	N	O	…
D	E	F	G	H	I	J	K	L	M	N	O	P	…
E	F	G	H	I	J	K	L	M	N	O	P	Q	…
F	G	H	I	J	K	L	M	N	O	P	Q	R	…
G	H	I	J	K	L	M	N	O	P	Q	R	S	…
H	I	J	K	L	M	N	O	P	Q	R	S	T	…
…	…	…	…	…	…	…	…	…	…	…	…	…	…

Figure 14 Encoding a message using a Vigenère table. In this example, the letter E of the message is matched with the letter C of the key, resulting in the encoded letter H.

For example, using the figure above, to encode the letter of the message E with the letter of the key C, you use the letter at their intersection of Column E and Row C, which is the letter H.

Let's see how Henry IV of France would have used the Vigenère cipher to encode the following message: "PARIS IS WELL WORTH A MASS" with the key "BOURBON." (He was the first king from the House of Bourbon.)

Henry would have used a Vigenère table to find the intersection of the column corresponding to the first letter of the message (P) and the first letter of the key (B), which yields the coded letter R. Then he would have done the same with the second letter of the message (A) and the second letter of the key (O), which yields P, and so on.

Once all the letters of the key had been used, he would have kept moving to the next letter of the message but started over with the first letter of the key. Can you work out for yourself what the encoded message would look like?[8]

Henry IV could thus have sent that encoded message to the Pope and, if the two of them had agreed on the secret key "BOURBON" during a previous in-person meeting, the Pope could decipher the message by shifting the letters in the other direction.

Introducing secret keys to encode messages was a brilliant idea: instead of having only 26 variants for the encoding and decoding process, you now had thousands. Before the age of computers, it made breaking a Vigenère cipher (decoding messages without knowing the key) a tiresome, sometimes even impossible task.

This new cipher shifted the secrecy from the protocol (as in Caesar's cipher) to the key, a word that could be chosen from among thousands of possibilities.[9] This meant that if you thought your key had been discovered by an enemy, you only had to replace it with a new one to keep communicating privately.

The Vigenère cipher's reputation as being "unbreakable" only grew with time. It wasn't until the nineteenth century that a general process would be devised that could break such ciphers. The technique used was based on a frequency analysis of the language used: for instance, in English, the most frequent letter is E, followed by T, and then A.

Breaking a Vigenère cipher was still a tedious task (before computers), but it became a manageable one. With enough resources, it could even be done quickly. During the American Civil War, the Confederacy used a similar

---

[8] The answer is RPMAUXGYTGDYDFVWVEC.

[9] Possible keys could even number in the millions if you allowed them to be made of two or three words put together.

encryption system, and many messages intercepted by the Union were successfully deciphered.

Let's pause for a minute to consider the fate of the Vigenère cipher. Breaking such a code went from being considered impossible to straightforward within a few centuries. The collapse started with the discovery of a new strategy (using statistical analysis of the English language) and accelerated once computers became available.

New techniques or available resources can often decrease the security of an encryption method; the safety of a particular cryptographic protocol is always a snapshot in time. Assumptions regarding the strength of cryptographic protocols, and by extension cryptocurrencies, must be framed by our current level of understanding and technology.

2.3 Enigma And World War II

Once the Vigenère cipher was considered "broken" (that is, easy enough to decipher), the method was once again improved. By using a series of evolving Caesar ciphers interspersed with permutations[10] of the alphabet, the Germans developed a powerful encoding weapon: the Enigma machine. This electro-mechanical machine was used daily during World War II.

Unbeknownst to the Nazis, the Poles had started to break some part of this cipher, and later shared their knowledge with the British army, who was able, thanks to a French spy, to decipher the keys used by Germans! Bottom line: sometimes it takes many different resources to break a code.

---

[10] Some letters were interchanged, while others stayed the same.

Up to this point in history, most of the decrypting work had been done by sharp (human) minds, sometimes assisted by machines, but the advent of computers would bring about a complete revolution in cryptography.

2.4 The Modern Era: Public-Key Cryptography

In the 1970s, as people started to use computers broadly across various industries and the military, they started to think of new ways to secure messages. One difficult problem encountered thus far in cryptography was that the keys had to be exchanged privately before secret communications could start. This was limiting, as communications between faraway interlocutors became more commonplace because there wasn't always an opportunity to meet in person beforehand.

How then could two people exchange messages, with confidence that they could not be decrypted by anyone else, without a prior exchange of keys?

Figure 15 Life before public-key cryptography.

A revolutionary idea started to emerge. Instead of exchanging a common secret key prior to the actual communication, each interlocutor could have their own set: a private key that would be known only to them and a public key that could be exchanged with others. In other words, everyone would keep their private keys secret, but the public keys would be known to all. Either one could be used to encrypt or decrypt a message.

Think of each one as both a padlock (when used to encrypt) and a key (when used to decrypt). The crucial trick here is that the public key opens the private lock, and vice versa. (See Figure 16.)

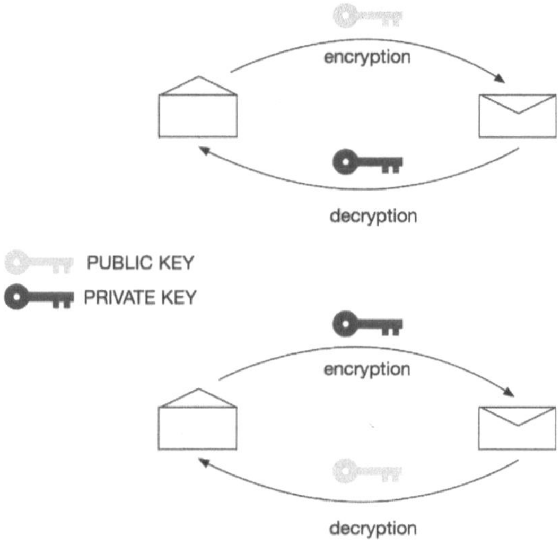

Figure 16 A message encrypted by either of the two keys can only be decrypted by the other one.

Imagine that Alyssa wants to send her friend Brandon an encrypted document. First she asks Brandon for his public key. Then she can encrypt her document with it and send the encrypted document to him by email. Once he has received it, Brandon (and only him) can decrypt it using his private key. (See Figure 17.)

Figure 17 Life with public-key cryptography: Alyssa encrypts her documents with Brandon's public key, and Brandon decrypts them with his private key.

This kind of protocol is known as *public-key cryptography* or *asymmetric cryptography* (because it uses different keys to encode and decode). To avoid confusion, I will refer to it as PubKey cryptography while leaving the term *public key* for the actual keys.

The revolution that PubKey cryptography brought allowed people like Alyssa and Brandon to exchange encrypted messages and documents even if they had never met or didn't even know each other.

2.5 Attempts At Breaking The Code

No cryptographic protocol is immune to attack. Imagine a malicious hacker, Charlie, has intercepted the encrypted document sent by Alyssa to Brandon. Charlie wants to decode the file, but he can achieve that in only two ways: by trying all different possibilities for the private key, or by stealing the key from Brandon.

The first strategy is for Charlie to try random keys until he finds the right one. This is called, in cryptography, a *brute-force attack*: no finesse to it and you're aiming to be exhaustive, not smart. Imagine attempting to open a padlock by trying all possible combinations. Time consuming, yes, but also straightforward.

The problem for Charlie is that Alyssa and Brandon can make this kind of attack ridiculously difficult by using longer keys. Let's say, for instance, that Brandon is using a private key of 10 characters, each one being a capital letter. For example, "LEUFCHSNCBP." There are 26 possibilities per character, so a key of length 10 can be any of 26x26x26x26x26x26x26x26x26x26 possible combinations. This number is usually written as 26^{10}. There are 26^{10}, or roughly 140 trillion,[11] possible keys to try.

If Charlie has 1 million computers, each capable of trying 10 million keys per second, it would still take him on average about 10 seconds to find the right key. Not bad at all, right?

Well, imagine now that Alyssa and Brandon decide to use keys that are 15 characters long instead of 10. The number of possible keys becomes about 2×10^{21} (a 2 followed by 21 zeros). That's an astoundingly large number, comparable to the number of grains of sand in all the beaches of the world. With the same setup as previously, Charlie would need about two and a half years to find the right key.

---

[11] A trillion is one thousand billion.

Better yet, let Alyssa and Brandon switch to 20 characters long keys. Then it would take Charlie 30 million years on average to guess the right key! The difficulty increases exponentially[12] with the key length.

But wait. Why "on average"? Let's say we have a jar filled with 99 red beans and 1 black one. We pick random beans out of the jar until we find the black one. We can be very lucky and pick the black one on the first attempt, or very unlucky and pick it on the last and one-hundredth attempt. Or we could grab it at any point in between. So *on average*, it will take 50 attempts before we find the black bean.[13]

Similarly, when Charlie tries to guess Brandon's key, he could get lucky and find it right away, although that is extremely unlikely. We can't say *when* Charlie would find the right key, but we can say that *on average*, it would take such a long time that Charlie probably wouldn't even want to bother!

If Charlie cannot guess the key, his only remaining strategy would be to steal it from Brandon. Any protocol that uses secrets is only as strong as the energy put into keeping these secrets private.

Fortunately, in the case of cryptocurrencies like Bitcoin, which relies on PubKey cryptography, the risk of having your secret keys stolen can be mitigated, for example, by using multisignature addresses, as I'll explain in Chapter 6. In that scenario, several private keys must be combined for decryption. This allows users to store different private keys in different physical locations, hence reducing the risk of theft.

---

[12] Exponentially means that for each additional character of the key, the number of possibilities is multiplied by a factor, which is 26 in our example.

[13] To be precise, in this example, the average would be 50.5 attempts. That's because the average is (1+2+3+...+100)/100 = 5,050/100 = 50.5 .

In sum, if Alyssa and Brandon use long enough keys and keep their private keys secret, they can exchange encrypted messages without any fear of being read. Encryption with long keys is so secure that its use in messaging apps was still the subject of legal debate in the US as of 2020.

2.6 Digital Signatures

Now that Alyssa and Brandon can send each other encrypted messages, how can Brandon be sure that the messages he receives are genuinely coming from Alyssa? Charlie could be sending forged messages to Brandon, pretending to be Alyssa. To do so, Charlie only needs Brandon's public key, and by definition that key is available to everyone. So how can Alyssa authenticate her messages so Brandon will know that she is the genuine sender?

If you were to suddenly ask your bank to empty your account and send every dollar to an unknown person at the other end of the world, they would be hesitant about this order and ask you to send a written letter with your signature, and maybe even a copy of your ID. And they would probably ask you security questions like your date of birth or your secret PIN (personal identification number). In other words, they can authenticate you as the sender by adding information that only you should possess.

The same can be done in PubKey cryptography, and in a much safer way.

Alyssa is the only person to know her private key, assuming it hasn't been stolen and she hasn't told anyone. She doesn't want to disclose it, obviously, but she can use that private key to encrypt a short message, for example, the current date, and put the encrypted date at the end of the message she writes to Brandon. So instead of sending this message…

`"I just bought 0.01 bitcoin. How about you?"`

She would send this one…

```
"I just bought 0.01 bitcoin. How about you?
bdca60ca1c45196bffe4b18"
```

This series of numbers and letters is the result of the encrypted send date. It's called the *digital* ***signature*** of the message. Now, as she did previously, Alyssa would encrypt the whole message above with Brandon's public key then send the encryption result to him.

When Brandon receives the encrypted message, he uses his private key, as before, to decode it. He can now read it clearly, except for the signature bit at the end. To check the signature's validity, Brandon decrypts the signature using Alyssa's public key and verifies that the result is the send date.

If the signature decrypts correctly, it proves that Alyssa (and no one else) encrypted it using her private key. If the signature is not valid (that is, it did not decrypt to the send date), the message could have been sent by anyone and the origin of the sender cannot be verified. (See Figure 18.)

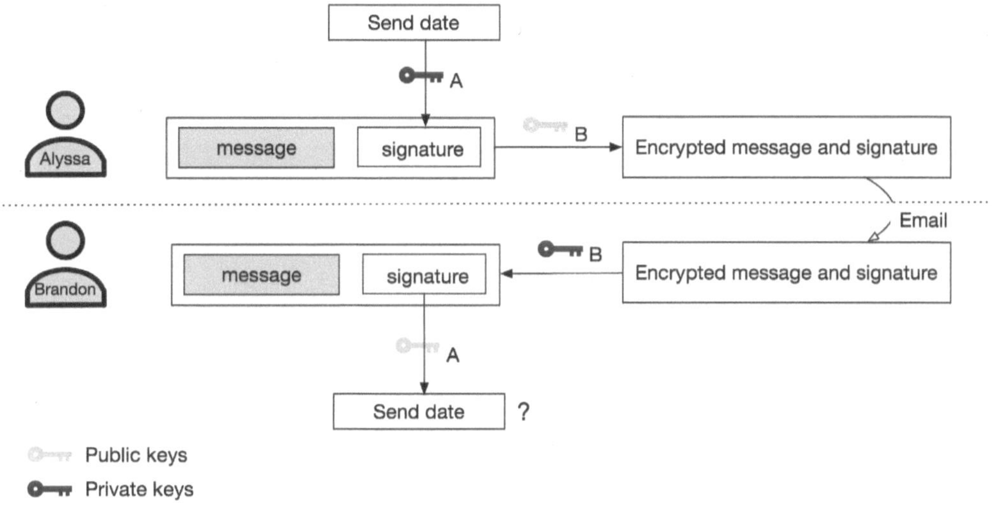

Figure 18 Top half: Alyssa adds a signature to her message before sending to Brandon. Bottom half: Brandon decrypts the message and checks that the signature is genuine.

Going back to our example above, can you spot a weakness in the protocol? Let's say Charlie has intercepted Alyssa's message to Brandon. Charlie now knows Alyssa's signature, which means he can copy it and reuse it to pretend he is her. As long as the date has changed, Charlie can send messages using Alyssa's signature, even though he doesn't know her private key. That's because, during any given day, the signature doesn't change.

But there is a solution.

To authenticate her message, Alyssa would encrypt the message itself with her private key, so the digital signature is computed from the content of the message. This way, when Brandon receives the digital signature, he will check that the signature decrypts to the content of the message.[14] In this case, there is no point in Charlie copying the signature because it will change with each new message. (See Figure 19.)

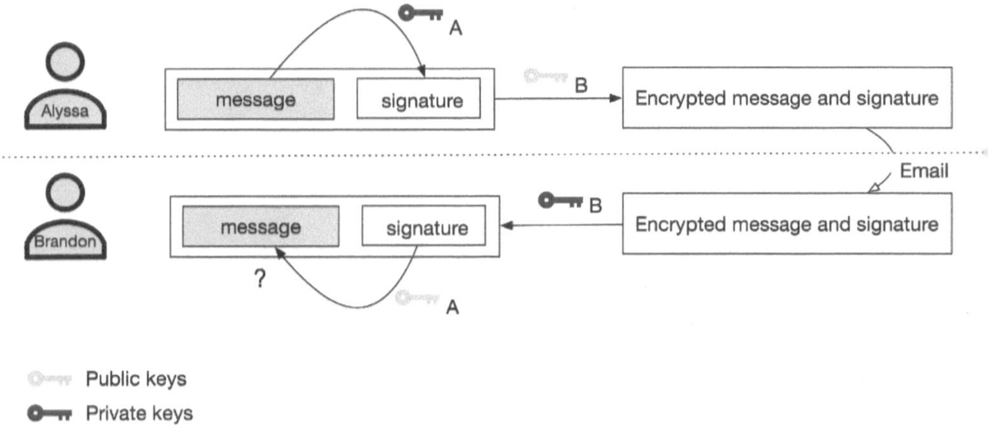

Figure 19 A better protocol: Alyssa signs the whole message with her private key. Brandon decrypts the signature with Alyssa's public key and confirms that it matches the message. Each new message has a new signature.

[14] This is still a slight simplification of the actual process but gives you the general idea.

Digital signatures play a major role in all cryptocurrencies. In Bitcoin, public keys are associated with addresses, which are where funds are held, while private keys are used to authorize the spending of these funds. Payments are authenticated using digital signatures. A digital signature provides proof that the sender of the payment is genuine, that they know the private key associated with the address where the funds come from, and are thus allowed to spend them.

But digital signatures are not limited to cryptocurrencies. Every time you connect to a secure website on the internet, your browser asks the website to authenticate itself through a digital signature scheme and verifies that the signature is valid. When you buy something on the internet by providing your credit card details, those numbers are transmitted in an encrypted way using PubKey cryptography. So essentially, without digital signatures, there would be no e-commerce.

2.7 Specificities Of Bitcoin

Going back to cryptocurrencies, PubKey encompasses a whole family of algorithms, so there are many ways to generate pairs of public and private keys. Bitcoin uses key pairs produced by an algorithm called ECDSA, for Elliptic Curve Digital Signature Algorithm. Bitcoin's creator probably chose it because it was already widely used in 2008 and was not under any commercial license. Besides, it was (and still is) considered very secure.

Bitcoin's private keys are 256 bits long, which means they use 256 characters when written with 0s and 1s. To make them more readable, they are usually displayed in base 16, using numerals from 0 to 9 and letters from A to F. This way, they only take up 64 characters. For example:

```
E9873D79C6D87DC0FB6A5778633389F4453213303DA61F20BD67F
C233AA33262
```

The number of possible private keys is 16^{64} (or 2^{256}), which is about 10^{77} (a 1 followed by 77 0s). This is an absolutely staggering number, comparable to the number of atoms in the observable universe. It makes Bitcoin's private keys completely immune to brute-force attack, where an attacker attempts to guess the right key by trying them all. A billion computers trying a billion keys per second would still require billions of years to figure out the right key.[15]

What's more, this gigantic number means the probability that two different Bitcoin users generate the same key is, in all practicality, nil. There is a similar chance for an average person living in the US to be hit by lightning *every single year* for 13 years in a row. And that would be very unlucky indeed.

As for public keys, they can be computed easily from private keys. Bitcoin does not, however, use public keys directly as addresses. Instead, each public key is put through another algorithm calling **hashing** to reduce its size to 160 bits (instead of 256), and the output of the hashing is the address corresponding to that public key. (See Figure 20.)

Figure 20 A private key is a random number; the public key is derived from the private key and the address is derived from the public key.

We'll come back to addresses and signatures in Chapter 4. But first, let us turn our attention to the magic of hashing.

---

[15] In reality, there are more private keys than addresses, which reduces the useful space of private keys to a still staggering 2^{160}, but the general conclusion remains.

Chapter 3

Hashes: The Fingerprints Of Digital Data

3.1 Human Vs. Digital Fingerprints

Human fingerprints start forming in the womb and are fully developed by the time an embryo is six months old. From then on, fingerprints can identify an individual for the rest of their life.

Fingerprints are one of a kind: two different people cannot have identical ones. Well, that's not entirely true. Some absolutely unrelated people can have remarkably similar fingerprints. It is an exceptional occurrence, however, so much so that in all practical matters it is considered impossible.[16]

Now imagine you are investigating a crime scene and you find some intriguing prints. You check the FBI database but find no match. Can the fingerprints by themselves tell you anything about the person they belong to? Absolutely not! Even though fingerprints identify a person uniquely, they

---

[16] Conversely, identical twins who share the same DNA do not necessarily have identical fingerprints.

cannot be "reversed" to uncover their owner. A fingerprint by itself does not reveal the sex, the age, the skin color, the height, or any other characteristic of its possessor. This is remarkable: fingerprints identify a person uniquely without giving away any information about them. (See Figure 21.)

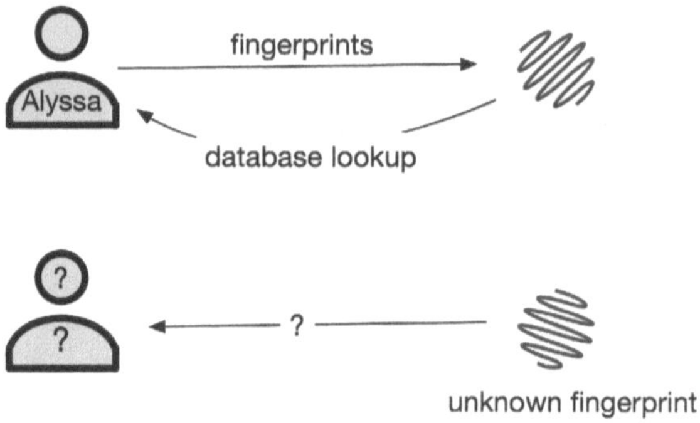

Figure 21 Alyssae's fingerprint is in a database, so it can potentially identify her. But an unknown fingerprint doesn't reveal anything about the person who left it.

What about data from our digital life? It turns out that digital files can be fingerprinted too. These digital fingerprints are called *hashes*. Hashes are short,[17] one-of-a-kind tags that can be produced quickly from any digital input. You can compute hashes for any kind of data, whether it's the whole text of *War and Peace*, a picture on your cellphone, a text message, or the entire content of your hard drive.

Most importantly, just like human fingerprints, hashes cannot be reversed. That is, given the hash of a digital file, there is no way to go from that back to the original file. You can't even tell whether you're looking at the hash of a text message or an entire encyclopedia. (See Figure 22.)

[17] Hashes are usually a few dozen characters.

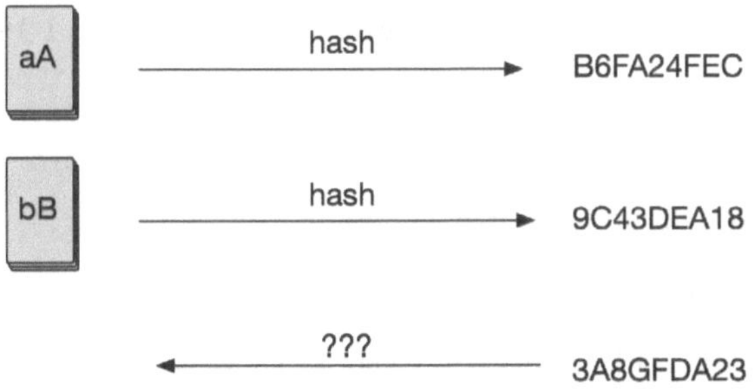

Figure 22 Each file has a unique hash, but a hash by itself doesn't reveal any information about its origins. Usually these combinations are a bit longer than the ones used in this example.

Thanks to their obfuscating properties, hashes, also called *hash functions*, are ubiquitous in Bitcoin. They are used for computing addresses and signatures, in the proof-of-work puzzles that miners compete to solve, and to chain consecutive blocks of transactions together.

3.2 Bitcoin's Hash Function: SHA-256

The kind of hashes used in Bitcoin is called *SHA-256* (pronounced "sha" as in "shark"). SHA-256 takes any digital input and computes a 256-bit output.[18] This output is usually displayed as a string of 64 characters. It is easier to read than a long series of zeros and ones, though it can still be a mouthful. SHA-256 is part of a family of functions that can produce hashes of different lengths, for example, SHA-512 or SHA-128.

What do SHA-256 hashes look like? Let's start with a very simple input such as the text "Today is Monday."

The SHA-256 hash of this input is…

---

[18] Digital information is measured in bits, which is the smallest possible piece of information, holding either a 0 or a 1. A byte is 8 bits. One megabyte, frequently used to describe the size of computer memories, is a little more than a million bytes.

1c729b249b61a429743e4f82fd9a6f253d09aea713947659f4d1c
a0e8ee3c66a

It's a string of 64 characters that seems utterly random.[19] Of course, it's not really random, it just looks that way.

You'll notice that once again, we're using numbers 0 through 9 and letters A, B, C, D, E, and F to present the hash: it's written in base 16. Whereas we humans are used to counting in base 10 (the decimal system), computers often use base 16 (the hexadecimal system), which is more suited to the binary nature of digital information.

Now let's see what happens if we change our input very slightly. Let's say we want to compute the hash of "Today is Monday!" where we've just replaced the period at the end with an exclamation mark. The new hash looks like this:

3ef829bc65c2283ab87be24cdaaf2cf90875072b27a03a0b8dfdb
4fda4819417

Even though these two phrases are identical except for one character, their hashes are quite different, as you can check by comparing them character by character.

Bitcoin uses this sensitivity to small changes for tamper protection. Any attempt to modify data in the blockchain will become immediately visible, not only in the block where the modification occurs, but also in all the following blocks. This is achieved through smart construction of the blocks and, in particular, the block headers.

---

19 You can check this hash by yourself. Look up "SHA-256 hash calculator" online.

3.3 Block Headers

In the blockchain, each block has two components: the header and the transactions proper. The header contains general information such as

- Time and date when the block was assembled
- A hash of the previous block's header
- A hash of all the transactions included in the current block (This hash is called the **Merkle root.**[20] See Figure 23 for an example.)
- A number called the **nonce**, which is a sort of counter used by miners

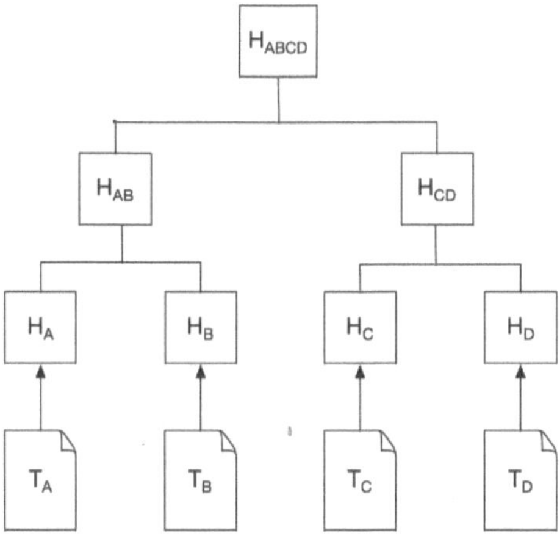

Figure 23 An example of a Merkle Tree. Four transactions (T_A to T_D) are displayed at the lower level. Just above them, their respective hashes are computed. Above those, hashes are put together by pairs and the hash of the pair is computed. On top, the Merkle Root, H_{ABCD} is computed from the pair just below.

[20] The name "root" references a data structure that resembles a tree.

Since the Merkle root hashes all transactions, any modification to them will be reflected inside the header, even though the transactions themselves are stored outside of the header. (See Figure 24.)

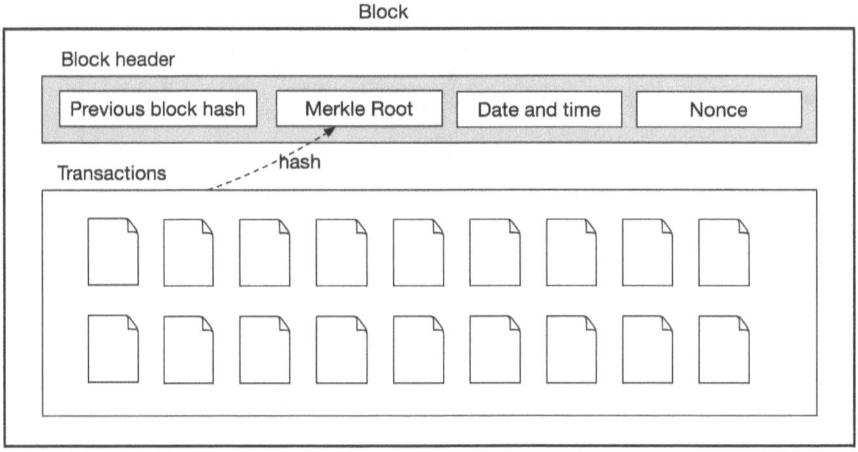

Figure 24 Block structure: The header does not contain a transaction, but it contains the hash of all transactions, which is known as the Merkle root.

Blocks can be identified in two different ways: by their height, which measures how far they are from the initial block, or by the hash of their header. For example, the genesis block, the very first block of Bitcoin's blockchain, is identified by its height of 0 or its header hash:

`000000000019d6689c085ae165831e934ff763ae46a2a6c172b3f1b60a8ce26f`

The second block, whose height is 1, can also be identified by its header hash:

`00000000839a8e6886ab5951d76f411475428afc90947ee320161bbf18eb6048`

In the header of each block, there is a copy of the previous block's hash. For example, the second block of the blockchain contains a copy of the genesis block's hash. Each block is connected to the previous one through the block hashes. (See Figure 25.)

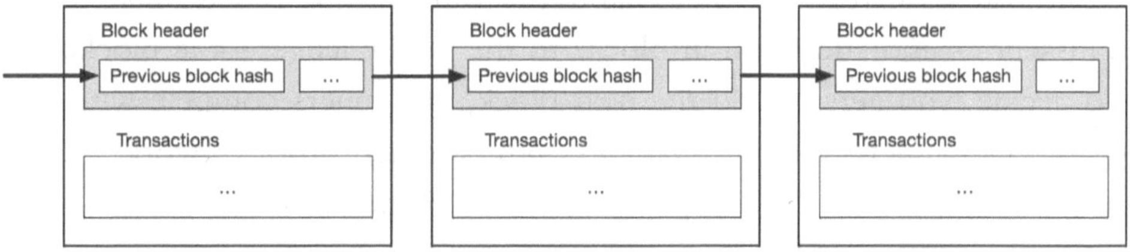

Figure 25 Each block contains the hash of the previous block. This way, a change in any block will cause changes in all subsequent blocks.

This connection brings a powerful tampering detection mechanism to the blockchain: any change inside a given block will create a change in the following block header, which in turn will provoke a change in the next block header, and so forth. Since Bitcoin nodes are continuously monitoring the validity of the chain of blocks, any tampering can be detected by a discrepancy in the header hashes. For example, if a node receives a block with an invalid hash, the node will reject this block and will not relay this faulty (or fake) block to other nodes. All honest nodes will do the same, ensuring that the faulty block does not belong to the blockchain.

Go back to the two examples of block hashes above; do you notice something peculiar about them? (hint: pay attention to how their first characters…)

They do not seem entirely random: both block hashes start with a string of zeros. In fact, every block hash of the Bitcoin blockchain begins with several zeros. This is not a coincidence but a built-in requirement. This makes it difficult (that is, time consuming) to build a block with a valid block hash, that is a hash starting with many zeros. This built-in difficulty is what makes the Bitcoin ledger secure, and its mechanism is called proof of work.

3.4 Proof Of Work: The Difficulty Of Finding Small Hashes

As you learned in the first chapter, in Bitcoin, the miners validate new transactions and add them in blocks to the public ledger—the blockchain. To decide who gets to add the next block, the miners compete with each other to solve a type of mathematical puzzle called proof of work, and the first one to solve the current puzzle gets to add their block.

To qualify as a valid solution for proof of work, a block hash needs to be lower than a certain number, which is called the **target**. In other words, it needs to start with a certain number of zeros.

Imagine that you are generating random numbers between zero and one million using a computer program. Your target is, for example, one thousand. This means that any number lower than 1000 is a winner. For example, 526034 is not a winner, but 000824 is. Any number you can write as 000### is a winner.

With a few subtleties, the idea is the same for Bitcoin mining. Miners try to form a block so that the block hash is lower than the target, and the first miner to find such a block wins and can add their own block to the blockchain.

Since the block hash is computed from the block header, the only practical way to get many different hashes is to vary the nonce.[21] The nonce's role is to provide a wide range of inputs for the hashing function without changing the other components of the header. (See Figure 26.)

---

21 Technically, the time could be changed too, but that would only allow one computation per second instead of the millions that can be done by changing the nonce.

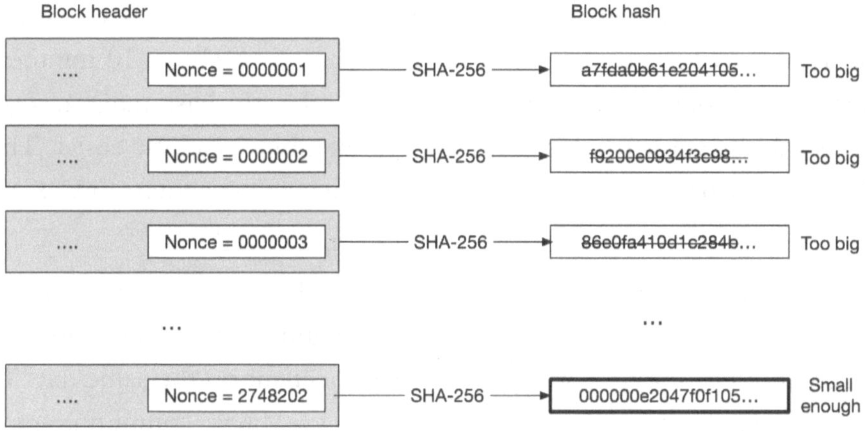

Figure 26 Proof of work: Trying different values for the nonce until the corresponding block hash is small enough.

It works like a lottery. Each new value of the nonce gives you a new ticket. To know if your ticket is winning, you compute the block header hash with that nonce value and see if the result is lower than the target. The more tickets you buy, the more chances you have to win (but also the more you have paid). Similarly, the more hashes you can compute within a given time frame, the more chances you have of finding a winning header hash before anyone else (but the more electricity you have spent doing so).

In the early days of Bitcoin mining, when there were only a few hundred or thousand people using their computers to mine, the target was quite high. This meant that it was relatively easy to find a winning hash, and hence to write a new block and get the block reward.

However, Satoshi Nakamoto wanted new blocks to be found, on average, every 10 minutes, regardless of how many people mined bitcoins.

To achieve that, every two weeks, the target adjusts automatically to match the computing power dedicated to Bitcoin mining. If in the two previous weeks, blocks have been found on average faster than 10 minutes, then the total computing power must have gone up and the target is lowered a bit, making the subsequent proof-of-work puzzles more challenging. Conversely, if the average time between winning hashes has gone above 10 minutes, it means that the total mining power of the network—the hash rate—has gone down, so the target is increased to make finding blocks a little easier. These automatic adjustments are in Bitcoin's code; they do not require any external intervention.

As of 2020, the target was extremely small, and the odds that a particular nonce leads to a valid hash were the same as winning the lottery with all six numbers in New York, New Jersey, and Connecticut on the same day! This incredibly small probability is balanced by the huge computing power dedicated all over the world to Bitcoin mining so that, all in all, a new block is still found on average every 10 minutes.

3.5 Inner Workings: Chop, Stash, And Mash

Let me give you a rough idea of how a hash function such as SHA-256 is computed using an example from the kitchen: making mashed potatoes.

This dish is easy to make: cook the potatoes, mash them, add butter and a bit of milk for that creamy texture. You can't go wrong. But, once a potato is mashed, there is no way to go back to the original potato. Mashing is a one-way action; it's not reversible. Hashing is the same, but with digital files instead of potatoes.

To compute hashes, functions like SHA-256 cut the original file into small bits, stash them together in a pile, and mash everything down. Then the process repeats: chop, stash, and mash. After a few rounds, the bits are so mixed together that there is no way to reconstruct the original file.

By carefully choosing how to cut the input file into small pieces and then stash and mash them, hash functions manage to produce short outputs that can be used to identify the corresponding unique inputs, similar to fingerprints.

You can also think of hashing like a paper shredder that always produces the same shreds from the same input. With a good paper shredder, you can't reconstruct the original sheet of paper from the shreds; there are just too many combinations.

Lastly, because hashes are of a fixed length, while their inputs can be of any length, it's inevitable that there are two documents somewhere with the same hash, just like two people can have (nearly) the same fingerprints. It's just extremely rare. In practice, finding such occurrences is so difficult that we don't have to worry about this issue.

For all practical purposes, hashes are unique tags. That's how I will use them now, as you learn how transactions are written in Bitcoin.

Chapter 4

Addresses And Transactions

Equipped with an understanding of PubKey cryptography and hashes, you can start looking at the accounting system used by Bitcoin. It's quite different from the familiar balances of standard bank accounts: the only data recorded by the blockchain are transactions, or movements of funds.

Bitcoin does not keep track of balances, but they can be inferred from the transitions. The blockchain keeps track of how funds are created (through mining) and how they are moved around.

4.1 Units Of Value: Bitcoins, Satoshis, And Pizza

America's monetary system expresses the value of goods and services in dollars and cents. In the blockchain, all values are expressed in satoshis, a tiny sub-unit that is worth one hundred-millionth of a bitcoin. That is, one bitcoin is worth 100 million satoshis (or "sats" for short).

As of January 2021, with the value of 1 bitcoin above 30,000 dollars, 1 satoshi was worth about 3/100 of a cent. Unlike the dollar, the bitcoin supply is limited by design: there will never be more than 21 million bitcoins in existence.

You may wonder, "Why 21 million and not another number?" Part of the answer is that 21 million is an arbitrary number that derives from three of Nakamoto's initial choices:

- To add a new block on average every 10 minutes
- To start with a block reward of 50 bitcoins
- To divide the block reward in two every four years

A new block every 10 minutes means 6 blocks per hour, 6 x 24 = 144 per day, which is roughly 210,000 blocks every four years. The first four-year cycle creates 50 bitcoins per block, the next one 25, then 12.5, and so on.

Since 50 + 25 + 12.5 + 6.25 + … equals 100, the process creates in total 210,000 x 100 = 21 million bitcoins.

As a result of this predetermined limit and in planning for a growing public adoption, Bitcoin's economy is ultimately a deflationary one: the supply is fixed, but the demand is supposed to increase over time. This means that the price of goods and services expressed in bitcoins should go down over time (assuming the success of Bitcoin's adoption).

For example, in 2010, software developer Laszlo Hanyecz participated in the first transaction exchanging bitcoins for something tangible: he bought two pizzas for 10,000 bitcoins. With Bitcoin's price around $30,000 in early 2021, he would only have to pay 0.001 bitcoin (or 100,000 satoshis) for the same order!

You might wonder why the sub-unit chosen for Bitcoin is so small. The reason is that the blockchain does not record amounts smaller than satoshis. For example 56.4 sats is not a valid amount; it has to be either 56 or 57. As a result, the satoshi unit had to be small enough that even if Bitcoin reached a million dollars or more one day, the satoshi could still be useful to price everyday things. In that scenario, a sat would be worth a cent ($0.01).

4.2 Bitcoin Addresses

The existence of bitcoins, as you may understand by now, is limited to the Bitcoin blockchain. In other words, you only own bitcoins if the majority of nodes say that you do. The blockchain, however, does not directly record who owns what. It simply records which address spends or receives bitcoins and how many.

Who owns a particular address is not a concern with Bitcoin. There is no explicit link between Bitcoin addresses and their owners in the blockchain. That is why Bitcoin is called *pseudonymous*: anyone could be the owner of a particular address.

Imagine removing all the names of people and companies that appear on your bank statement and replacing them with numbers. The result would be very confusing. That is precisely the sort of information the blockchain provides.

To add to the (intentional) confusion, Bitcoin users can have as many addresses as they want. So while it is not impossible to make credible assumptions about who owns which address(es), the task can be significantly challenging.

However, given a particular Bitcoin address, it is straightforward not only to compute how many bitcoins are "stored" at that address, but also to get a history of all transactions that have used it. In terms of privacy, anyone who knows (or can discover) your Bitcoin addresses knows your financial history. Therefore, keeping their addresses private is a major concern for most Bitcoin users.

So what do Bitcoin addresses look like? Addresses are strings of characters—similar to a bank account number, but using both letters and digits—where bitcoins can be stored. To send or receive bitcoins, you need such an address.

How can you get one? Well, you don't really *get* an address; you *make* one. Here's how, at least in theory:

1. First, you generate a random 256-bit–long number. The result is your private key.[22]
2. Then you multiply your private key to find your public key. This multiplication is of a special kind called *elliptic curve multiplication* and it cannot be reversed, which means that even if someone knows your public key, they wouldn't be able to guess your private key.
3. Finally, you hash your public key using two different kind of hashes to find your public address.

The result of the second hash is only 160 bits long. It's the Bitcoin address associated with the private and public keys. Only the owner of the address's private key can spend the funds stored at this address. (See Figure 27.)

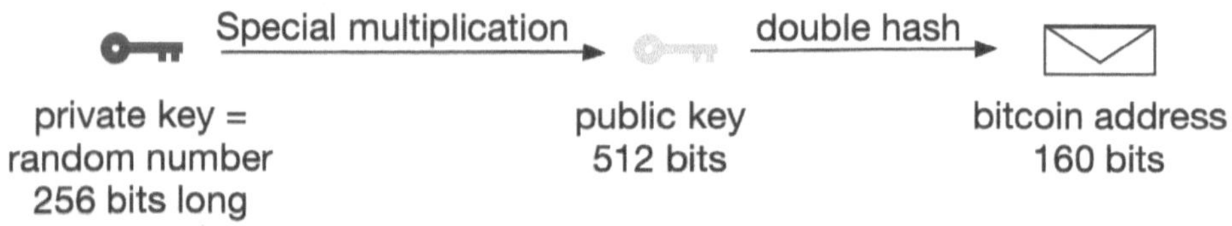

Figure 27 A public key and address are generated from a random private key.

[22] There is a constraint on the private key, but almost all randomly generated numbers will satisfy it.

If that sounds complicated (it is), do not worry: in practice, you don't need to generate the keys and address by yourself. Any bitcoin wallet, whether on your laptop or your phone, can do that for you. I'll explain in Chapter 6.

What do addresses look like? These 160-bit numbers are usually written in the more presentable form of a string of 30-something characters. For example, rather than writing this…

```
1100001101010010010101101011101010001010011010101010001
0000001100100001101100100101111010011000101100000001010
0111100010111000001110101101110100000101000101000111 0
0101001000010111101110000100000000
```

…it's much easier to write the same Bitcoin address as…

`1JomQQYZCxbpPrRVKf69hsfyNiGgDqTLv3`

The allowed characters include the digits plus lowercase and uppercase letters. However, to reduce visual ambiguities, Bitcoin addresses do not use the number zero, uppercase letters O or I, or lowercase L (l). This kind of address is called *Base58* because it uses 58 possible characters (9 digits + 25 lowercase + 24 uppercase).

Here are two more examples of Bitcoin addresses.

- `1A1zP1eP5QGefi2DMPTfTL5SLmv7DivfNa`

That's the genesis address, the one used by Satoshi Nakamoto in the first Bitcoin transaction, the creation of the first 50 bitcoins. Single-owner addresses usually start with "1" as they require only one signature for the spending of funds.

- `3KCkZbx7UwaUotMj1FWA5ApLVrJupHuX2k`

This one is a multisig address, one that is owned jointly by several people, similar to a joint bank account. Multisig addresses start with "3" instead of "1" and require multiple signatures to allow funds to be spent.

As you can see from these examples, Bitcoin addresses look very much like random chains of characters. You've seen this before: this seeming random-ness is a result of hash functions.

However, not every string of characters of the right length and format is a valid Bitcoin address. If you typed a random string of characters that looks like a Bitcoin address, there would be less than one chance in a billion that it would be a valid Bitcoin address.

Likewise, if you typed a genuine Bitcoin address but made a couple of mistakes while typing it, then in more than 99.999% of cases it would not be a valid address. If someone tried to use it to send to or receive funds, it would be rejected by the network. This feature prevents people from accidentally sending funds to nonexistent recipients.

To prevent these types of mistakes, Bitcoin addresses are sometimes presented as QR codes rather than strings of characters.

QR (Quick Response) codes are square barcodes that were invented in Japan in the 1990s for the automotive industry, but have since become ubiquitous. Many mobile wallet apps and software programs automatically provide these alongside any Bitcoin addresses they use. However, you should note that websites that propose to generate such QR codes from a given address are usually highly suspicious: most of them are scams that will generate a QR code linked to their own Bitcoin address instead of the one you typed! (See Figure 28.)

Figure 28 QR code for the genesis address.

Bitcoin addresses are like wallets: containers to store your coins. But they are locked. Addresses can be unlocked using the private key that was used to generate them. And some addresses (multisig addresses) need several keys to unlock their funds.

In Bitcoin, since there is no central authority that assigns addresses, you can generate as many different ones as you need. And it is generally a good practice to use a new address every time you receive funds. It makes tracking your bitcoins more difficult, hence increasing your privacy. This is usually done automatically by the software or app wallet you use.

Generating a new private key and address is free and easy to do with the right app or software. It is also worth noting that generating Bitcoin addresses does not require access to the Bitcoin network, or even to the internet. It can be done entirely offline. Only the transfer of funds requires online access.

You can generate a new Bitcoin address using software on your laptop (digital wallets), on your phone (mobile wallet apps), or through hardware wallets. As mentioned above, most app or software wallets handle addresses and private keys automatically. (You'll learn more about software and hardware wallets in Chapter 6.)

The idea that funds can actually be "stored" in a place as virtual as Bitcoin addresses seems confusing at first. But it's not so different from using a credit card online. The money is not really in your credit card; it's accounted for in the ledgers of the card company. And the knowledge of the card numbers and three digits on the back are the keys that allow spending of the funds.

The difference lies in how this spending is authorized: by a central authority in the case of credit cards, by the decentralized network of nodes in the case of Bitcoin. And by the way, the use of private keys makes Bitcoin incredibly more secure than using a credit card online.

One way that Bitcoin addresses are significantly different from bank accounts is accessibility. Anyone, without providing any form of identification, can generate a multitude of Bitcoin addresses to receive, store, and spend funds. There is no central or even local authority to decide who can or cannot have a Bitcoin address, which means that literally everyone can transact with bitcoins.

4.3 Transactions: Inputs And Outputs, Spent And Unspent

Now that you know what addresses look like, I'll show you how to use them to move funds.

Imagine you're buying a newspaper at a stand. You choose the one you want, take out coins and bills, and hand them to the merchant. Now if the newspaper you're buying costs $1.50 but you only have a $5 bill in your wallet, you know you cannot physically cut the $5 bill and give that to the merchant. Instead, you have to hand over the whole $5 bill and get some change back, say three $1 bills and two quarters.

Bitcoin works somewhat similarly. You cannot "cut" the digital coins held in your Bitcoin addresses; you have to use them for their full value. For example, say you have a coin worth 5.00 bitcoins and you want to use it to pay for something costing 1.50 bitcoins. You cannot cut your 5.00 bitcoins and use just a part of it. Instead, you can send a payment for 5.00 bitcoins and pay two beneficiaries with it: the merchant for 1.5 bitcoins and yourself for the change, that is 3.5 bitcoins. (See Figure 29.)

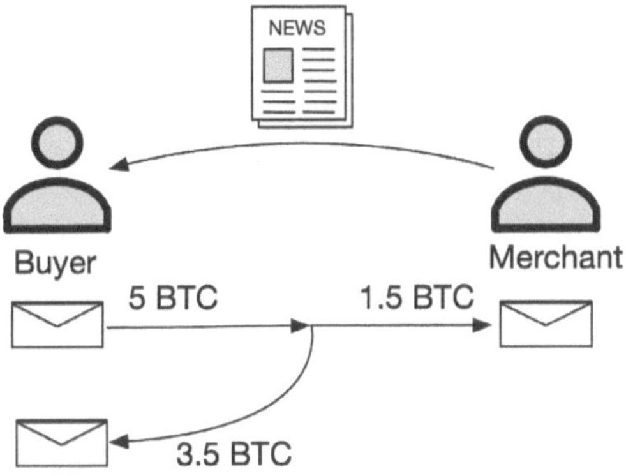

Figure 29 Buying a (very expensive) newspaper with bitcoins. You use a 5 BTC coin, pay the merchant 1.5 BTC and send 3.5 BTC back to another one of your addresses.

In the case of Bitcoin, however, you are not paying the merchant the whole 5 BTC and then asking for change, as you would do with cash. Instead, you are authorizing the payment of 1.5 BTC[23] to the merchant and of 3.5 BTC to yourself, using a 5 BTC coin. You do not need the merchant's approval to get your change.

Another difference is that Bitcoin does not work in fixed denominations as cash does (where bills can only be $1, $2, $5, $10, $20, and so on). Bitcoin coins can be of arbitrary value, not just round numbers. For example, you

[23] BTC is a widely used abbreviation for bitcoin.

could pay using a 4.289123 Bitcoin coin, if that's what you have at your address, and receive a 2.789123 Bitcoin coin as change.

Going back to our newspaper example above, you can think of this payment as a box with two sides. On one side, you have the input, the 5 BTC coin you're using to pay; on the other side, you have the outputs, the 1.5 BTC going to the merchant and the 3.5 BTC going back to yourself. In fact, any Bitcoin transaction[24] works like this: it has inputs (the coins you're paying with) and outputs (where the payment goes and how much). (See Figure 30.)

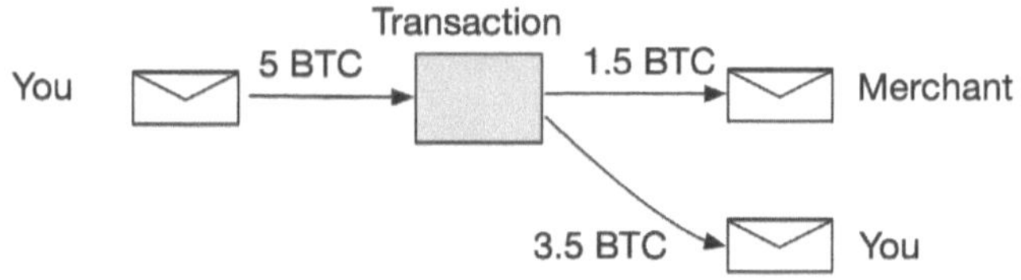

Figure 30 The previous transaction: it has one input (left side) and two outputs (right side).

4.4 The UTXO Database

Every Bitcoin payment, such as the one described above, consumes some coins as inputs and creates new ones as outputs. That's why Bitcoin coins are called *unspent transaction outputs*, or **UTXOs** for short: the "live" coins are the ones that have not yet been consumed (or destroyed) by a payment.

Each node of the Bitcoin network keeps track of these live coins in a UTXO database.[25] Every time a transaction is written into the blockchain, the nodes update their database by removing the transaction inputs (the coins consumed) and adding the transaction outputs (the coins created). The

[24] I use "payment" and "transaction" interchangeably in the rest of the book.
[25] A database is simply a collection of records, usually accessible by a computer software.

UTXO database is not part of the blockchain; it is something that has to be recreated by each node from the data contained in the blockchain.

This database is used, for example, to check against double-spending. An incoming transaction's inputs must all be in the current database to be valid. Meeting that requirement means that the transaction is only using live coins. If, however, some input cannot be found in the database, it means that the transaction is trying to spend a coin that either never existed or has already been spent. As a result, such a transaction would be rejected.

4.5 Transaction Fees

Another requirement for a valid Bitcoin payment is that it does not create more value than it consumes. So a transaction cannot create bitcoins out of thin air! On the contrary, most transactions create a little less than they consume. The difference is called the **transaction fee**, and it goes to the miner who first includes that transaction in a successful block. (See Figure 31.)

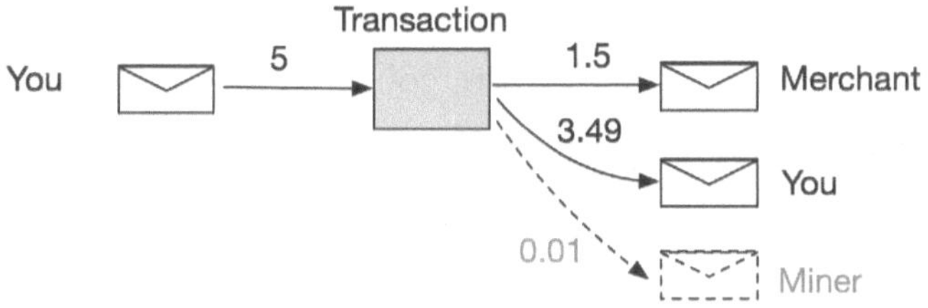

Figure 31 A payment, including transaction fees.

Transaction fees incentivize miners to write each new transaction into the next blocks. When a new payment is received by the Bitcoin network, it is not written immediately into the blockchain. Instead, each miner puts it into its **mempool**, a waiting room for transactions. The higher the fee a person is willing to pay, the quicker their transaction will be picked from the mempool and mined into the blockchain.

Transaction fees form a typical supply-and-demand market, and as such they vary widely over time. For example, in 2020, they went as low as $0.10 per transaction and as high as $5.

Note that transaction fees depend on how much space the transaction takes up within the blockchain (since miners try to collect as many transactions as possible in a block), but that they do not depend on the amount being transferred. Paying $5 when you are moving $1 million would be extremely cheap, but the same fee becomes exorbitant when applied to a $10 payment. It's an issue that Bitcoin developers are trying to address, and I'll come back to that later.

4.6 A More Complex Transaction Example

Let's go back to the transaction format and see what more you can do. Say you want to pay your friend Brianna two bitcoins and your friend Chloe one. Brianna provides you with one of her Bitcoin addresses for the payment and so does Chloe. You look into your Bitcoin addresses and find three coins (UTXOs) that you are going to combine to pay your friends.

- Your Address A stores a 1.0-bitcoin UTXO and 0.75-bitcoin UTXO
- Your Address B stores a 1.5-bitcoin UTXO

That's a total of 3.25 bitcoins, which is enough to pay both your friends and send back some change to another one of your addresses, say Address C.

Instead of sending two distinct payments, Bitcoin allows you to write a single payment to multiple beneficiaries: you just add more outputs to the transaction, as illustrated in Figure 32.

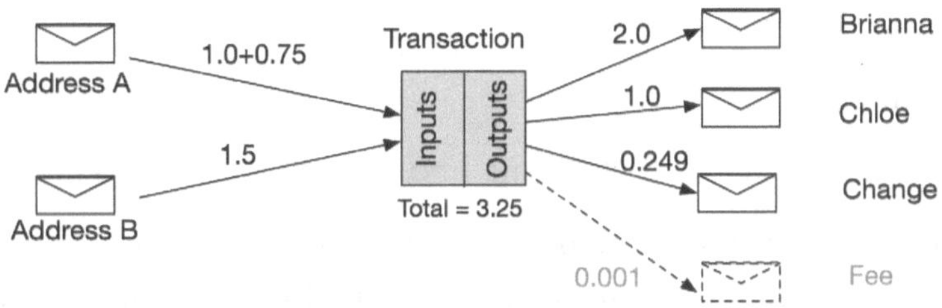

Figure 32 A transaction from multiple addresses to multiple payees.

Note that the miner's fee, which is 0.001 bitcoins in the example above, is not explicitly specified in the transaction. The reason is that you don't know which miner will eventually write your payment into the blockchain, so you can't specify in advance which address you want the fee to go to. Instead, the fee is expressed implicitly by the difference between the inputs and the outputs. It is collected later by the winning miner in what's called the **coinbase transaction.**

4.7 Coinbase Transactions

In general, each transaction must have at least one input and one output. Bitcoins are not created out of thin air: new UTXOs are only created by consuming old ones.

The exception to this rule is that the first transaction of each block is allowed to create an output (a new UTXO) without consuming any input. These coinbase transactions accomplish two goals: creating the block reward and collecting the transaction fees.

The first transaction of any block is always the coinbase transaction. As miners gather transactions from the mempool, they assemble them into a tentative block and add a coinbase transaction at the beginning. This transaction adds the fees from all the transactions in the block to the current block reward, and sends the total to an address that belongs to the miner.

For example, it can look like this:

```
Input: none
Outputs: 6.36187426 bitcoins to 1MUz4VMYui5qY1mxUaocc
```

In that particular example, the block reward was 6.25 bitcoins. Remember that the block reward is set automatically by the bitcoin code and is cut in half roughly every four years. It went from 12.5 bitcoins to 6.25 bitcoins per block in May 2020.

The transaction fees collected in the example above were…

6.36187426 - 6.25 = 0.11187426 bitcoins

…a much smaller sum than the block reward.

As block rewards decrease over time, the incentive they create is supposed to be replaced by the collection of transaction fees. So far, however, miners have been earning money mostly from block rewards, transaction fees being a much smaller part of their income. It remains to be seen whether relying increasingly on transaction fees is viable in the long run, or whether this will lead to fewer miners in competition, which could endanger the security of the network or to an increase in transaction fees. Which scenario will prevail depends largely on the evolution of Bitcoin's price.

In the next chapter, we'll be looking at digital signatures in Bitcoin transactions, which is how Bitcoin checks that coins are only being spent by their rightful owners.

Chapter 5

Signatures: Authenticating Payments

5.1 Signatures: Checking Valid Ownership

In the previous chapter, I described a transaction as the transformation of inputs into outputs, or as the destruction of some UTXOs and the creation of new ones. While this is true, there is still a crucial aspect to consider: the authentication of the spender.

Each input UTXO can only be spent by its legitimate owner. To authorize the spending of a UTXO, a user must prove that they know the private key corresponding to the address holding the UTXO. As you learned in Chapter 2, the way to do that is to use digital signatures.

Thus, a Bitcoin transaction will contain not only a list of input UTXOs, but also a digital signature for each of these inputs. For each input, the signature must be signed by a private key that unlocks the corresponding address. Remember that it is easy for an outside observer to check whether a signature is valid: one only needs to use the corresponding public key to decrypt it. (See Figure 33.)

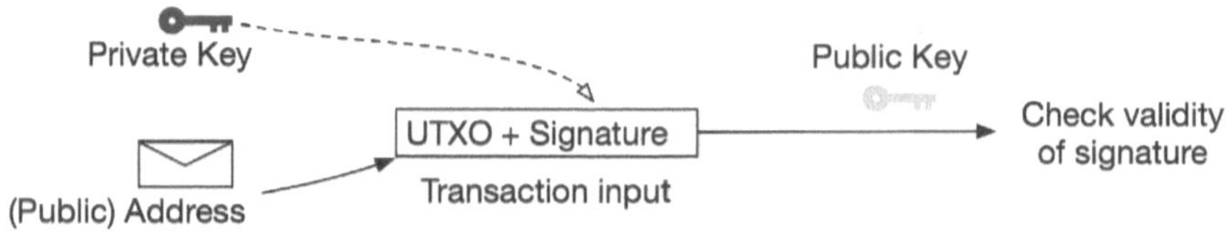

Figure 33 Verifying a signed transaction input. Note that the private key is never divulged; only the digital signature it produced is published.

Let's take a simple example. Say you want to pay your friend Victoria one bitcoin. For the sake of simplicity, assume that you just happen to have a one bitcoin UTXO in one of your Bitcoin addresses. (We'll forget about transaction fees for now.) The payment will have just one input and one output and will look like this:

```
Input: 1 BTC from Address1 with Signature1
Outputs: 1 BTC to Address_Victoria
```

Anyone on the network can see your payment and check that the signature is genuine. For example, Victoria herself can check the signature's validity by using your public key. Since you're the only one who knows your private key, the fact that your public key can decrypt the signature proves that the transaction was indeed signed by you.

I have illustrated this transaction in Figure 34.

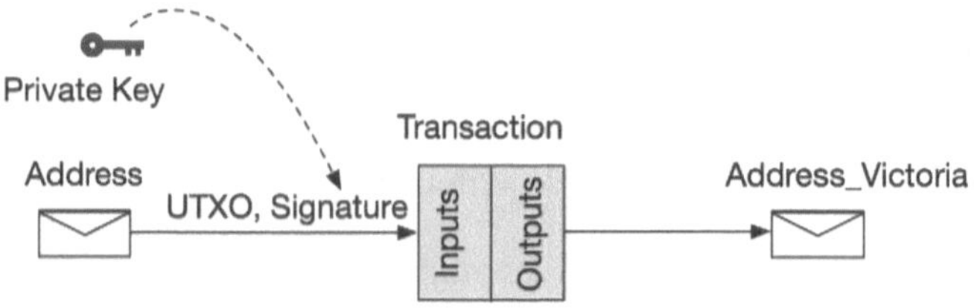

Figure 34 A signed transaction. The private key is NOT part of the transaction; only the signature is.

Note how the private key is *not* part of the transaction; it is only used to sign the spending of the input UTXO. The private key is never divulged, so it is safe. What's more, the signature that you provide for this payment is only valid for the spending of this particular UTXO. Even if you have more coins stored at the same Bitcoin address, signing a transaction spending one of your coins does not put your other coins in danger. No one can reuse your signature to spend a different UTXO.

In the case of a more complex transaction, say one with multiple inputs and outputs, the signature scheme is the same: each input must be signed by a private key that controls the corresponding address.

Furthermore, to prevent any tampering, signatures reference not just their input but the transaction as a whole. For example, it would be problematic for a payment to sign only its input because then anyone could alter the outputs and still have a valid signature. Instead, each signature is computed from all inputs and outputs of a transaction, making it impossible to alter any data or, for example, to redirect funds to an unintended recipient.

5.2 Bitcoin Script: Locking And Unlocking Of Bitcoins

I have described transactions as transforming UTXO and signatures into new UTXOs. This is still a slightly simplified model. In reality, both the inputs and the outputs contain short pieces of computer code called **scripts**. The goal of these scripts is to "lock" or "unlock" the bitcoins being transferred.

For example, when we say that we want to move some bitcoins to a particular address, what we mean is that these bitcoins should be "locked" to that address. When this occurs, they cannot be moved again unless someone provides a signature (corresponding to that address) to "unlock" them. Thus, the input and output of each transaction can be seen as the unlocking and relocking of coins.

- Inputs: unlocking coins that were previously locked
- Outputs: locking new coins to recipients' addresses

Consider a succession of simple transactions, each using only one input and one output, and transferring the same amount from Alyssa to Brandon to Chris. This sequence is illustrated in Figure 35.

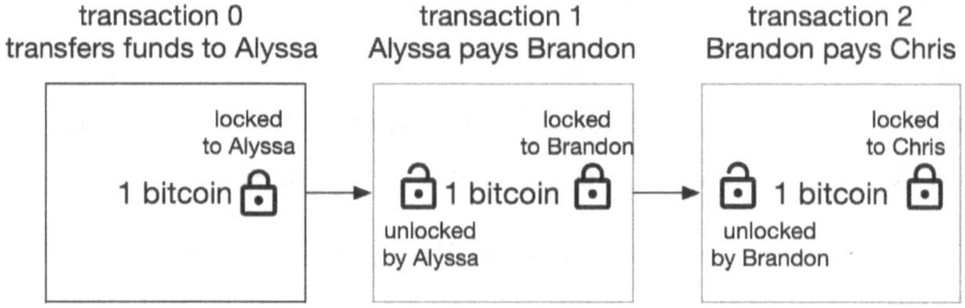

Figure 35 Each transaction unlocks the funds, moves them to a new address, and locks them there.

The first transaction transfers the funds to Alyssa and locks the coin to her Bitcoin address. The second transaction unlocks the same funds using Alyssa's signature and sends them to Brandon, locking it to his Bitcoin address. The last transaction unlocks the funds using Brandon's signature and transfers them to Chris, locking it to his address.

Each transaction "moves" bitcoins by unlocking them from one address and locking them to a new address. The unlocked coins are spent (UTXOs being consumed), while new locked coins are created (UTXOs being created).

So how do scripts enable the locking and unlocking of funds? Consider the example above where the first transaction locks bitcoins to Alyssa's address. The **locking script** will consist of these details:

- Alyssa's address
- Instructions to check that a signature and public key correspond to that address

The locking script does not contain Alyssa's public key, nor does it contain a signature produced from Alyssa's private key. It only contains her address and code instructions.

In the next transaction, Alyssa is moving her coin to Brandon. To authorize this spending, she will provide, in the **unlocking script**, the two following elements:

- Her public key
- Her signature

Any node on the Bitcoin network can then verify the payment by putting the unlocking script of Transaction 1 with the locking script of Transaction 0 and checking that the two scripts together run smoothly. As a result, the following two conditions are checked:

- The public key provided in Transaction 1 can be hashed into the address provided in Transaction 0
- The signature and public key provided in Transaction 1 match (in other words, the public key can be used to decrypt the signature)

(See Figure 36.)

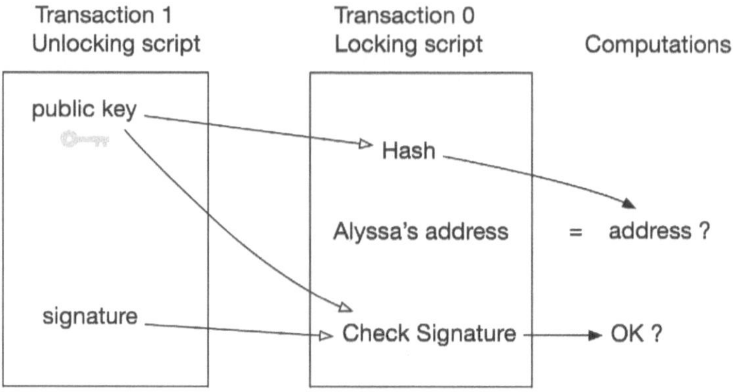

Figure 36 The data from the new transaction is fed to the script of the previous transaction. The two scripts together verify that the public key is correct and that the signature is valid.

The kind of script used to lock funds in this example is the most commonly used type of payment in Bitcoin. More than half the transactions use it. It's called Pay-to-Public-Key-Hash, or P2PKH, because it allows the funds to be locked to the *hash* of a public key rather than to the public key itself.

This is an additional precaution used in order to hide the actual public key until the moment when the funds are spent. This extra layer of hashing also provides added protection against quantum computing. Quantum computers are machines that rely on "guessing" the right solution to a problem rather than trying all potential solutions. However, these computers are still experimental and will not be a threat to Bitcoin's security at least for the next few decades.[26]

Pay-to-Public-Key-Hash is one of several types of scripts that can be used to make payments in Bitcoin. The important idea is that Bitcoin allows a

---

[26] See my story "Cryptocurrencies: finding comfort in (very) large numbers" on medium.com/@meyer.raph for more details.

limited number of programming keywords, or operations, that can be included in a script. This coding language is very basic and has been limited by design in order to ensure that running the scripts is always fast and never results in an infinite loop, for example.

Bitcoin's scripting language is, however, the founding idea behind **smart contracts**: the delivery of payments when some conditions (that can be verified automatically) are met. This idea has been developed much more thoroughly in the Ethereum blockchain, a rival cryptocurrency that focuses on smart contracts and decentralized applications.[27]

5.3 Multisignatures

Transaction scripting opens up possibilities for more complex locking mechanisms. In particular, it allows for **multisignatures**, where bitcoins can be locked to addresses that must be signed by multiple users, but not necessarily all of them.

For example, if you have a joint bank account with your partner, either of you can initiate a payment: only one signature is required. This would be called a **1-of-2 multisig** in Bitcoin. Scripting generalizes this possibility to any number of signees. For example, the board of a company might require a majority to allow certain spending, so that if five people sit on the board, three votes are necessary. In Bitcoin, this kind of constraint can be implemented by a **3-of-5 multisig**: any three signatures (out of five) can allow a transaction to go through.

Multisig can be implemented through a different kind of locking script, called Pay-to-Script-Hash, or P2SH. Unlike P2PKH, which requires a public key and signature to unlock, P2SH can use any code for unlocking. P2SH

---

[27] See Ethereum.org, the official website for Ethereum.

locks funds to a particular hash: the unlocking script must hash into that particular value to be valid. This little trick allows the locking of bitcoins to any combination of conditions while keeping the size of the locking script small.

In the case of a P2SH implementing a multisig, the number of signatures needed is not revealed until the funds are unlocked. Before that, only the hash of the script is published in the blockchain, not the content of the script itself.

For example, in a **2-of-3 multisig**, Alyssa, Brandon, and Charlie can lock funds together. Spending funds will require any two of them to sign. That allows Alyssa and Charlie, for instance, to spend funds even without Brandon's approval. (See Figure 37.)

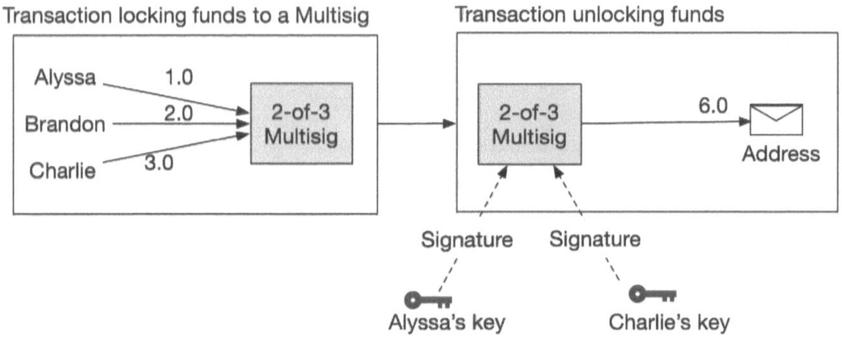

Figure 37 A 2-of-3 multisig is used to lock funds by Alyssa, Brandon, and Charlie. When Alyssa and Charlie decide to spend these funds, they don't need Brandon's approval because only two signatures are required.

Strictly speaking, the multisig "address" to which funds are locked is not actually an address (a public key hash) but a script hash. This kind of address can be recognized in the blockchain as starting with a "3" rather than a "1" for P2PKH addresses.[28]

Multisig address are extremely useful for improving the security of storing bitcoins. They can also be used in escrow situations.

5.4 Multisig For Escrow

Imagine that Alyssa wants to buy a used laptop from Bruno, but she's never met him and hence doesn't know whether she can trust him. In particular, she doesn't want to pay him before she has received the laptop and checked that it works correctly. Similarly, Bruno doesn't trust Alyssa and he does not want to send his used laptop to her before he can be certain that she has indeed committed the funds to pay him. What can Alyssa and Bruno do to resolve this situation?

Even though they don't trust each other, they could agree to trust another person, say James, to be their judge in case of a disagreement. In that case, instead of sending a payment directly to Bruno, Alyssa can send a payment to a 2-of-3 multisig where the three participants are: herself, Bruno, and James. This way, she has committed the funds without paying Bruno directly.

Once Bruno sees that Alyssa has made this payment, he knows that she cannot get the funds back by herself, so he can confidently send his used laptop to her. When Alyssa receives Bruno's laptop, she can check that it works correctly. If she's satisfied with her purchase, she signs a payment to Bruno from the multisig. Bruno just needs to add his own signature to make the payment valid.

---

28 At least that was the case until 2017 and the SegWit "update," which I'll explain in Chapter 9.

What happens if the laptop doesn't work as expected? Then Alyssa can call on James to decide who's right. If James decides that Alyssa is right and Bruno is in the wrong, he can sign a payment from the multisig back to Alyssa, which Alyssa can sign as well to get her funds back.

On the contrary, if James rules that Alyssa is in the wrong and that the laptop seems fine, he can sign a payment from the multisig to Bruno, who will then cosign in order to get paid.

See Figure 38 for a visual of how the three different scenarios play out.

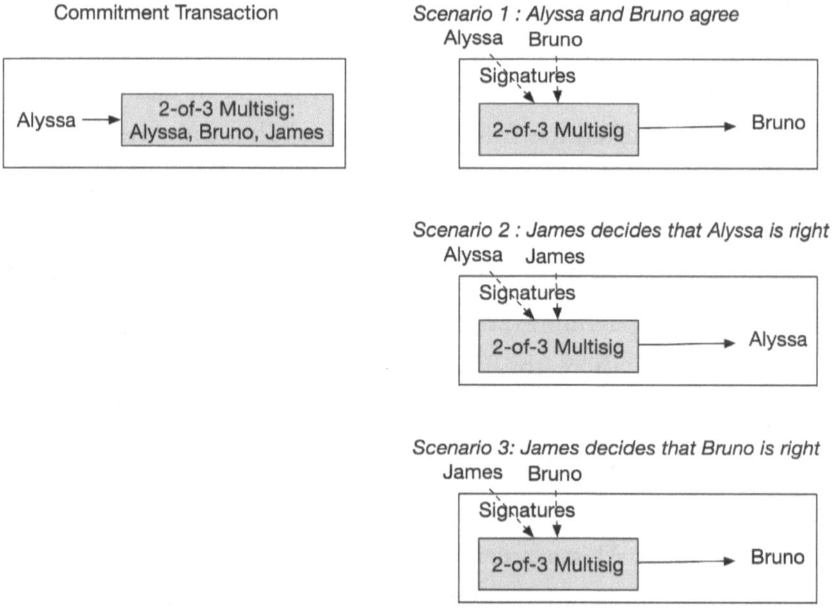

Figure 38 Left: Alyssa puts some funds in escrow. Right: Three different scenarios to recover the funds.

By making James the judge of their potential disagreement, Alyssa and Bruno can both be protected against fraud. Note that James only intervenes if there is a problem; otherwise, Alyssa and Bruno can conduct their transaction without interacting with him, except for the creation of the multisig address. Finally, note that James cannot run away with Alyssa's money; he would need either Alyssa or Bruno to sign in order to make a payment to himself.

Now that you have seen what occurs inside a Bitcoin transaction, you're ready to see how these transactions are added to the blockchain. In the next chapter, you will learn more about the mining process and how transactions are confirmed.

Chapter 6

Mining: Adding Transactions To The Blockchain

In the previous chapters, you learned what Bitcoin addresses are and how bitcoins are transferred from one address to another. We've identified bitcoins as digital coins—UTXOs, or unspent transaction outputs.

Now we're going to take a step back to look at the larger picture: how transactions are added to the blockchain through mining, and how the blockchain prevents tampering with these transactions. To do that, we need to start with a reminder of why Bitcoin is different from previous digital currencies.

6.1 Before Bitcoin: Consensus In A Centralized Network

Bitcoin is not the first digital coin. It takes inspiration from several projects such as eCash (1993), e-gold (1996), and Liberty Reserve (2006). You may remember from the first chapter that the essential obstacle any digital money must avoid is double-spending. That's because when coins and bills are replaced by digital code, duplication becomes a trivial task, and therefore checking against double-spending becomes necessary.

To solve this issue, all precursors of Bitcoin adopted the use of a centralized ledger. Before accepting a digital coin, a merchant needed to check with a central authority that this coin had not already been spent.

This is similar to what happens when you get cash from an automated teller machine with your debit card. The ATM connects to a central authority (your bank) to verify that there is sufficient money in your account before delivering it. In other words, there is a consensus—an agreement—about the status of your account: all actors of the financial network (such as other banks and ATMs) can refer to your bank to check your balance. (See Figure 39.)

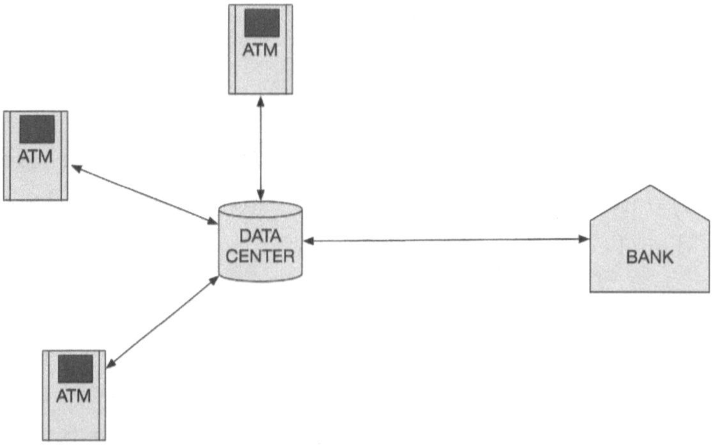

Figure 39 Taking out cash with a debit card. All ATMs connect to a data center to check the balance before delivering money. The data center is updated by the bank, which is the central authority.

One reason the precursors of Bitcoin failed is because they were using this centralized model. It made their central ledger a constant target for hackers. In computer security terms, this type of weakness is called a *single point of failure* because hacking the central ledger would allow someone to take control of all the money.

Between the systemic weakness of a central ledger and the fact that these digital currencies attracted criminals drawn to the layer of anonymity, these early attempts at digital coins either went bankrupt or were forced to close by law enforcement agencies. But their failings inspired Satoshi Nakamoto to take things in a different direction.

6.2 Bitcoin: Consensus In A Decentralized Network

When Nakamoto designed his digital money, he switched things completely: instead of relying on a central authority to keep track of coins, users of Bitcoin relied on each other. There is no central ledger anymore, but a multitude of ledgers that are maintained by participants of the network. Every participant keeps track of all the coins. Everyone is responsible for maintaining their own copy of the ledger.

Not only is the Bitcoin ledger distributed,[29] it is also transparent. Unlike with the centralized banking model, anyone can read transactions. This transparency is not a weakness; on the contrary, it provides security. If everyone can see what's going on, they can reveal fraud much more easily. It is for the same reason that retail bank locations usually have clear glass windows: in case of a robbery, passersby can see the action from the street and call the police.

Making the ledger distributed means that there is no longer a single point of failure. Attacking a single participant, or even several of them, does not bear any fatal consequence: the ledger can be recovered from all the other participants. That makes this model highly resistant to hacking.

---

[29] "Distributed" in this context means that there are many copies of the ledger, which are scattered throughout the network.

But distributing the ledger to all participants comes at a price: in the absence of a central authority, who are we supposed to trust? If two peers disagree on whether a coin has already been spent, for example, how do we know which one is telling the truth? In other words, how do we achieve consensus in a distributed environment?

This problem is difficult to solve. It is an instance of a well-known mathematical puzzle known as the *Byzantine Generals Problem.* Imagine an army, led by a number of generals, besieging a city. The generals are spread around the city and they must decide on a common strategy; namely, whether to attack or retreat, solely by exchanging messages.

The problem is that some generals are traitors, but no one knows how many or who they are. Can the (loyal) generals still reach a common strategy without being derailed by the traitors?

Similarly to how the Byzantine generals must reach a consensus about their strategy, the nodes of the Bitcoin network need to reach a consensus regarding the ledger: they must all agree on which transactions are part of it and which are not. And they must reach this consensus even in the presence of some possibly dishonest peers.

The Bitcoin protocol provides a probabilistic solution to this problem. Assuming there are more honest peers than dishonest ones, a consensus can be reached if peers decide, when faced with different versions of the blockchain, to always keep the longest one—that is, the one with the most blocks.

For example, say you are a new node (participant) in the Bitcoin network. You just joined, so you don't yet have your own copy of the blockchain, the Bitcoin ledger. How do you get one? You simply start asking other nodes, your neighbors, for their copies, which you download block by block.

Each time you download a new block, you can verify that it is valid by checking the block header: it must contain the hash of the previous block and can be hashed itself so that the result is smaller than the target (as explained in Chapter 2). That's what proof of work is about: making block header hashes small, which we know takes time to do but is quick to check.

At first, all your neighbors agree on the blocks you are asking for. But at some point, you may have two neighbors who disagree on what the next block is. This discrepancy may be because one of your neighbors is malicious, or it could just be because you've reached the current end of the blockchain and the ledger hasn't reached a stable state yet.

You then have to choose between two different "tails" of the blockchain. (See Figure 40.) So which neighbor do you trust?

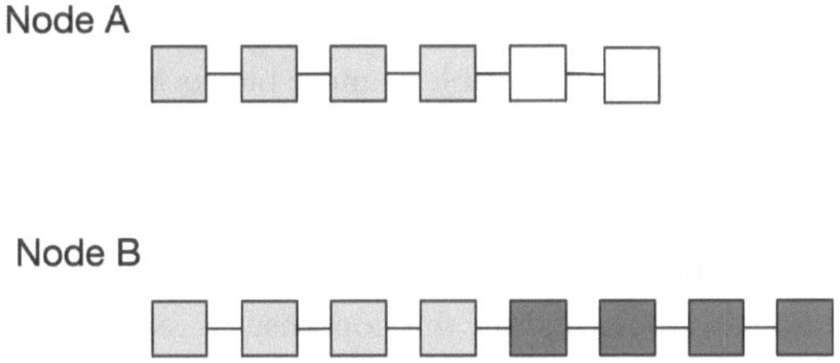

Figure 40 Nodes A and B disagree on the blockchain. In the absence of a central authority, the longest chain is considered to be the genuine one.

The solution is to keep asking for the following blocks. At some point, one of the two chains will be longer than the other; that's the one you should keep. Why? Because the more valid blocks that are included in a chain, the more computing time has been spent solving proof-of-work puzzles, therefore the more difficult it is to forge that chain. The longest-chain rule tells you to keep the chain that is the most difficult to make, because it is the most likely to be genuine.

The longest-chain rule provides a probabilistic solution to the consensus problem: the further back you look into the blockchain, the more confident you can be of its content. In other words, a block that has had 100 blocks added on top of it is almost a certainty, while a block that just got added or that has just one or two blocks on top of it could still be discarded from the blockchain in the future. With blocks, older is better: the older a block is in the blockchain, the more immutable its transactions have become.

In the distributed context of Bitcoin, reaching consensus means attaining a network state where a majority of nodes agree on what constitutes the blockchain. The majority of nodes must agree on the current sequence of blocks, and therefore which transactions are in the blockchain and in which order. By doing so, Bitcoin protocol protects against double-spending because a fraudulent transaction will be rejected by the majority of nodes. On the contrary, a transaction that is valid and added to the blockchain becomes more and more immutable as more blocks are added on top of it.

6.3 Who Are The Miners?

Now that you understand that reaching consensus is important to prevent double-spends, let's focus on how this consensus is reached by adding blocks of transactions to the ledger. This is the work of the Bitcoin miners. But who are they?

Bitcoin is a peer-to-peer network, and its participants are called *nodes*. Anyone can join or leave at any time since there is no central authority regulating the network.

If you want to become part of the Bitcoin network, all you have to do is download software that will connect you to it. The most common one is Bitcoin Core (see bitcoin.org). The software simply establishes a connection with other nodes and downloads a copy of the blockchain from them while verifying it block by block, transaction by transaction.

When the initial download is complete, you become a full node, which means that the software keeps your copy of the blockchain up-to-date and relays new transactions and new blocks to and from other nodes. It's very hard to determine how many people are running this type of software, but it was estimated, as of 2020, that there were at least 10,000 full nodes in the Bitcoin network, and probably many more.

Initially, Satoshi Nakamoto thought that every node would also be a miner. Why wouldn't people who participate in the network want to earn money for it? But as mining equipment got more and more efficient (and expensive), miners became a small, specialized group inside the Bitcoin network. Unlike "simple" nodes, miners add new transactions into tentative blocks, search for proof-of-work solutions, and get to add their blocks to the ledger when they find valid solutions. And as you learned, they receive the block reward and transaction fees corresponding to those blocks.

Miners are the corporate actors of the Bitcoin network: they work for profit. Nonmining nodes work for free, but their efforts are still essential. They make sure miners are honest by checking that every new block added to the blockchain follows the Bitcoin rules. Even if all miners were to conspire to cheat, the regular nodes would reject their blocks. So both roles are important to the health of the Bitcoin network.

6.4 How Are Transactions Added To The Blockchain?

As you've already learned, for a transaction to be valid, it must satisfy several conditions.

- All its inputs must be in the current unspent outputs (UTXO) database

- Each input must have a valid signature or unlocking script
- The transaction must not create more bitcoins than it consumes (except for coinbase transactions)

Even regular (nonmining) nodes check the validity of transactions. They reject blocks that contain invalid transactions or refuse to relay transactions that are not valid. But miners also gather transactions and try to add them to the ledger.

Consider a new Bitcoin payment by Alyssa. Let's see what happens step-by-step.

First, Alyssa needs her transaction to reach the miners. Whether through a mobile app, a full node, or an online service, this transaction is sent to at least one Bitcoin node. This node will check that the transaction is valid (that is, does not violate Bitcoin's rules) before relaying it to their neighbors.

From node to node, Alyssa's transaction is propagated throughout the network until it reaches several miners. Each miner who receives it puts it in a sort of waiting room called the **mempool**. (See Figure 41.)

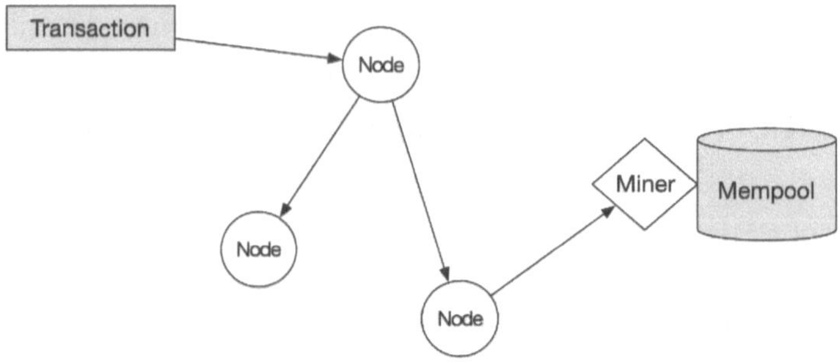

Figure 41 A transaction finding its way to a miner's mempool.

When the miner has time, they can pick up Alyssa's payment from the mempool. How quickly Alyssa's transaction is picked up is mostly determined by its transaction fee, as miners can only put a limited number of transactions in a block. Note that what really matters is the fee per length: a transaction that occupies more space needs a higher fee to attain the same priority. That's why transaction fees are usually expressed as satoshis per byte.[30]

When a miner picks up Alyssa's transaction, they bundle it with other pending transactions to form a block, stuffing as many transactions in as the maximum block size allows. Once a tentative block is formed, the miner starts computing the corresponding block header hash for different values of the nonce, until the hash is smaller than the current target. That's the proof-of-work loop, which is repeated billions of times until a solution is found.

The first miner to find a valid block hash (a solution to proof of work)—let's call him Adam—can claim to add his own block to the blockchain. To do this, Adam will send his block, complete with his proof-of-work solution, to his neighbors. If valid, the new block will be propagated throughout the network, each node adding it to their own copy of the blockchain.

When other miners receive Adam's block, they give up their own proof-of-work computations, add Adam's block to their blockchain, then start new proof-of-work computations based on the updated chain of blocks. (See Figure 42.)

[30] Or satoshis per vbyte for SegWit transactions. (See Chapter 8.)

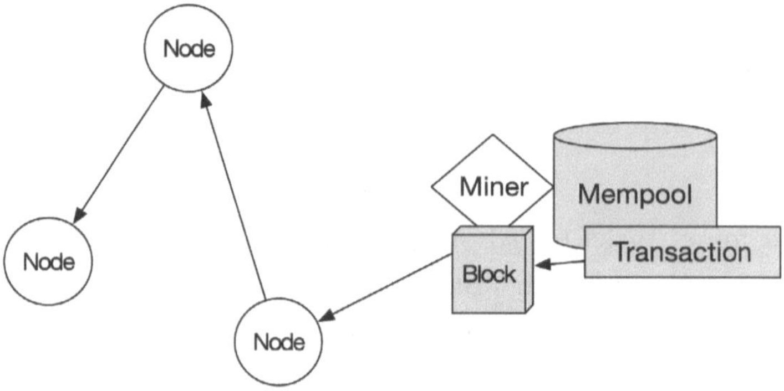

Figure 42 A newly mined block being propagated through the network.

When most nodes have updated their copies of the blockchain to include Adam's block (and hence Alyssa's transaction), that transaction is said to be confirmed. More precisely, it has received one **confirmation**.

As more blocks get added to the blockchain on top of Adam's, the confirmation of Alyssa's transaction increases accordingly. For example, if three additional blocks have been added to the blockchain, the transaction is said to have four confirmations. As the confirmation number increases, the transaction becomes more and more immutable. In other words, the possibility of Adam's block not being ultimately part of the blockchain becomes more and more remote.

6.5 Mining Ties And How They Are Broken

Since miners are in competition with each other, sometimes two different miners will find a winning block hash within seconds of each other[31]. For example, say Adam and Brenda have both found a nonce that gives them a winning hash almost at the same time. Because information does not travel instantaneously within the network, Adam has already started propagating

---

[31] This happens naturally every few weeks.

his winning block when he finds out that Brenda also has a winning block, and vice versa. What happens then?

Some nodes will receive Adam's block first, while others will receive Brenda's block first. But most nodes will, in time, receive both. So how do they choose which one to keep? At this point, the longest-chain rule does not apply because both chains—the ones ending with Adam's block and the one ending with Brenda's block—are of the same length. Adam and Brenda are in a tie.

To break the tie, nodes simply wait for the next block to be mined. Each miner, upon receiving the news that a competitor has found a new block, adds this new block to their copy of the blockchain and starts mining "on top" of that block. Thus, a miner who receives Adam's block first will put that in their blockchain and form a new block on top of that one when looking for a proof-of-work solution. And vice versa if they received Brenda's block first.

When a new block is found, say by miner Clara, then one of the two tied-in blockchains becomes longer than the other. If, for example, Clara mined a block on top of Adam's, then the blockchain ending with Adam's and Clara's blocks becomes the longest chain, and hence all nodes will switch to that chain and forget about Brenda's block. The tie is broken. (See Figure 43.)

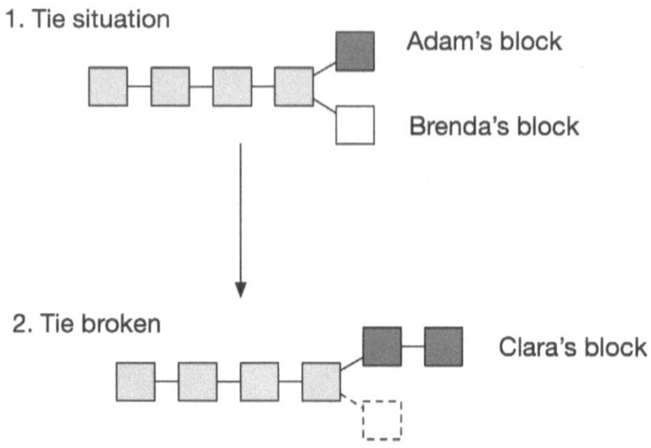

Figure 43 Top: Two blocks found at the same time create a tie. Bottom: The tie is broken when the next block is found.

6.6 Mining Attacks

This tie-breaking situation described above does not imply any malice; it is bound to happen naturally from time to time. However, the longest-chain rule could be exploited by a malicious attacker under certain circumstances.

In Bitcoin, there are not many ways to cheat. For example, you cannot create bitcoins out of thin air, change the recipient address of someone else's transaction to steal their funds, or even alter the number of bitcoins that someone is sending you. That's because any of these actions would result in an invalid transaction, which would be rejected by all honest nodes of the network and therefore would not end up in the blockchain.

Additionally, you cannot spend bitcoins that don't belong to you because spending is protected by signatures, and forging a signature is impossible unless you know the private key. Again, an invalid signature would immediately be detected by the honest nodes of the network and the corresponding transaction would be rejected.

One of the ways you *can* try to cheat, however, is by forging an alternative blockchain—in particular one that does not contain a payment you've already made to someone. Let's look at an example.

Say Brian has agreed to pay Chloe 100 bitcoins in exchange for $1 million in cash. (The reason for considering such huge amounts will become clear soon.) Before Chloe gives him a briefcase filled with $100 bills,[32] she wants to know that his bitcoin payment has been confirmed by the network. To be safe, Chloe is going to wait until Brian's payment has received a couple of confirmations before releasing the briefcase.

But let's say that the deal is done: Brian walks out with the cash, and Chloe has received a confirmed payment in bitcoins.

As soon as Brian sends the payment to Chloe, he can also instruct some miners to start mining (in secret) an alternative chain that does NOT contain this payment. His hope is that once he walks out with the briefcase, he will be able to convince the Bitcoin network that the real blockchain is the one that does not contain this payment. This way, Brian would keep both the cash and the bitcoins.

However, all honest nodes are going to follow the Bitcoin protocols, and in particular, the longest-chain rule. So if Brian wants his fake chain to become the real one, that chain needs to become longer than the genuine blockchain. In other words, the miners working for Brian must produce a longer chain than the genuine one before releasing it publicly. The tricky thing to understand here is that while Brian's blockchain might be fraudulent, it still needs to follow the protocols, and in particular it must contain correct

---

32 Did you know that $1 million in $100 bills takes up roughly the inner space of a microwave oven?

proof-of-work solutions. Therefore, producing such a chain is resource-intensive.

A simple calculation shows that if Brian doesn't control 50% of the network's mining power, his chances of producing a longer blockchain quickly go to zero.

So the only sure way for him to mine a longer chain is to control at least 50% of all the mining capacity of the Bitcoin network. That's because it assures him that on average, *his* miners are going to find proof-of-work solutions faster than the rest of the miners. And eventually, Brian will be able to publicly release a blockchain that is valid, does not contain his 100-bitcoin payment, and is longer than the genuine one. Therefore his chain will be accepted by all nodes.

Now, taking control of half of the Bitcoin miners is no small feat. It is going to cost a lot of electricity, and certainly a lot of money, to pay the miners to do the dirty work. In 2020, Bitcoin mining as a whole consumed on average eight gigawatts of electricity (a typical nuclear power plant produces around one gigawatt). Even at cheap prices, controlling half of that would cost an attacker at least $100,000 per hour in electricity alone. Add the cost of renting the computers and the price jumps to $300,000 per hour.

Due to their cost, such majority attacks only focus on transactions involving lofty amounts, which is why their targets are always cryptocurrency exchanges and never individual users. So far, no such attack has ever been attempted successfully in Bitcoin, but smaller rival cryptocurrencies have witnessed successful attacks (Bitcoin Gold, for example). The more computing power dedicated to mining, the more costly it becomes to launch a majority attack (also called a *51% attack*).

These attacks can be somewhat difficult to understand, but here's the main takeaway: Bitcoin makes cheating very expensive. In practice, 51%

attacks are not a concern anymore for the Bitcoin network. The hash power of Bitcoin (the total computing power dedicated to mining) makes it too expensive to attack its blockchain.

6.7 Confirmations In Practice

How can we use this information in practice? Say Brielle wants to buy a software license from Charles using bitcoins. In the previous chapter, you saw how multisignatures allow the use of escrow in transactions. But here Brielle and Charles want to interact directly, without using an escrow.

Charles wants to make sure that Brielle's payment has gone through before sending the license keys. How can he do that? Simply by checking the blockchain to see whether her transaction is confirmed.

At first, Charles will see Brielle's payment appear as unconfirmed: this means it has been received by the network but is still in the mempools.

After 10 or 20 minutes, however, the payment should be picked up and mined into a block. At that time, it becomes confirmed. This reassures Charles that Brielle's payment is valid and is not a double-spend. But as you saw earlier, having one or even two confirmations does not necessarily mean that a transaction is completely immutable yet. A longer alternative chain could still replace the current blockchain, either because there is a tie or because of a 51% attack led by Brielle to recover her funds.

The cost of such an attack increases with the number of confirmations the block being attacked has received. So for an amount equivalent to a few hundred dollars, waiting for three or four confirmations is regarded as very safe. It would be extremely foolish to organize a 51% attack just to reverse a $100 equivalent transaction. For an even smaller amount, such as a few dollars, waiting for just one confirmation should be enough.

Sometimes, you may not even need to wait for a confirmation; just seeing the transaction in the mempool can be enough to reassure you. This is similar to how most people don't check that every dollar bill or quarter they are given is valid. It's all a question of risk: the larger the amount in the transaction, the more confirmations you need before considering that the funds have indeed been transferred irreversibly.

In our example, Charles may be satisfied when Brielle's transaction has received three confirmations before he delivers the software license. If Charles were selling a house instead of a software license, he would probably want to wait for five or six confirmations instead.

The number of confirmations you want to see is not fixed: it must be adapted to the amount being transferred. The higher the amount, the more confirmations you need. Of course, more confirmations means more waiting time—on average, 10 minutes per confirmation. (See Figure 44.)

Amount in $	$1	$10	$100	$1,000	$10,000
Number of confirmations	0 or 1	1 or 2	2 or 3	3 or 4	5 or 6
Approximate wait time	Seconds to 10 minutes	15 minutes	30 minutes	45 minutes	60 minutes

Figure 44 Reasonable number of confirmations to wait depending on the amount being paid,

Consider this: while it is impractically long to wait 10 minutes for a payment to go through when buying a cup of coffee, it is rather efficient to wait only an hour when transferring millions. In this regard, one can say that Bitcoin was really built for moving around large amounts efficiently and securely, but not to pay for small everyday items.

I'll address this limitation (and others) in Chapter 9, but since you now have a good understanding of Bitcoin's basic features, let's focus on the more practical aspects, such as buying and storing funds.

Chapter 7

Practical Matters: Buying And Storing Bitcoins

Now that you have a better understanding of the technology underlying Bitcoin, let's take a short break from the theory to dive into the practice. In this chapter, you'll learn how to buy (and sell) bitcoins and how to store them securely.

7.1 How To Buy And Sell Bitcoins

In the early days of Bitcoin, the only way to obtain bitcoins was to participate actively in the network by becoming a miner: you would receive new bitcoins from the block rewards. Since 2013, however, with the advent of ASIC[33] machines (computer units specialized in solving proof-of-work puzzles), mining has increasingly become a professional industry. And even though mining bitcoins is still technically possible on your laptop or desktop

[33] ASIC stands for application-specific integrated circuit, computer hardware built specifically for a particular purpose: in this case, Bitcoin's proof of work.

computer, the competition from professional miners means that you will not earn a significant number of bitcoins this way, if any.

Since earning new coins is now the domain of industrial miners, bitcoins must be acquired from people who already own them. The most popular way to buy bitcoin is through cryptocurrency exchanges. Exchanges are the trading places of cryptocurrencies. In the US, some of the most well known (as of 2020) are Coinbase, Gemini, Bitstamp, and Kraken.

Any of these exchanges can be used by US customers to buy bitcoins with dollars, and all of them request some form of identification, as required by Know Your Customer (KYC) laws.[34]

If you are comfortable with providing your identity, this is the easiest way to buy bitcoins (or other cryptocurrencies). Cryptocurrency exchanges are similar to stock brokers: they put buyers and sellers in contact so that, for instance, bitcoins and US dollars can be traded. Once you have an account with an exchange and have provided them with a way to fund your account, either through a credit card or bank account, you can easily buy and sell bitcoins.

The experience is similar to buying stocks: the exchange gives you a rate (number of dollars for a bitcoin) and you can decide how much you want to buy or sell at that rate. There are limits to the amounts you can trade within a day or a month, but they increase significantly when you provide sufficient identification.

Exchanges are also **custodial**. This means that they hold the private keys to the bitcoins you buy. In other words, the exchange you are using is the actual owner of the bitcoins, but it keeps a balance sheet in your name.

---

[34] KYC guidelines are part of the USA PATRIOT Act of 2001; see resolution H.R. 3162.

This makes it easy for users to "buy" bitcoins, but it also presents a risk: if the exchange is hacked,[35] you could lose some of your funds. Hence the popular maxim in the Bitcoin community: "Not your keys, not your bitcoins."[36] This means that by letting the exchange manage your private keys, you are leaving the actual funds in their hands and trusting them to keep your funds safe. Indeed, ownership in Bitcoin is equivalent to knowledge of the private keys.

To mitigate this counterparty risk, a common strategy for users is to transfer any bitcoins bought on an exchange to an external address they own as soon as the funds are available in their account. This forces the exchange to release the coins to a wallet that's under your control (meaning that only you have the private key). With this mitigation strategy in mind, exchanges remain the easiest way to acquire bitcoins (or other cryptocurrencies). When you want to sell, you just transfer back from your wallet to the exchange.

Buying on an exchange and transferring to a personal wallet (especially a hardware wallet) is the strategy I recommend for anyone investing more than a hundred dollars in cryptocurrencies. In the next section I will explain what is a hardware wallet, how they work and why they have become the preferred method of storage.

Bitcoins can also be bought directly from individual sellers, whether online or in person. Sites like LocalBitcoins.com provide such a service by matching buyers and sellers based on their location. Unlike with exchanges, every seller can set their own rate, and amounts are usually limited to a few thousand dollars.

---

35 Unfortunately, this happens regularly, especially with the smaller exchanges.
36 This saying was popularized by Andreas Antonopoulos.

Some sellers will ask for a form of ID (depending on the amount you buy), as sellers who do not verify the identification of buyers for large transactions could be accused of money laundering. To ensure the safety of both buyers and sellers, these sites usually use an escrow mechanism. Payments in dollars are made through several instant methods, such as Zelle or PayPal.

Finally, bitcoins can be bought through special ATMs. Instead of delivering cash, these machines allow you to buy bitcoins and deliver them to any address you provide (for example by scanning a QR code of your address). Rates tend to be higher than through exchanges. Even for small amounts, a form of registration is usually necessary, for example providing your full name and phone number. For larger amounts, you may need to have a picture of your ID taken by the machine.

Once you own any kind of cryptocurrency, you can trade it for a different cryptocurrency. For example, you can buy ETH (Ethereum) for BTC (bitcoin) or sell BTC for XRP (Ripple). A lot of cryptocurrency investors use this to diversify their portfolio: holding a mix of different coins can bring down its volatility. Some exchanges focus on crypto–dollar pairs, while others specialize in crypto-to-crypto pairs.

7.2 Storing Bitcoins: Hot And Cold Storage, Software And Hardware Wallets

Bitcoin wallets are, in their simplest form, a collection of public and private keys. The public key works like an account number where you can receive funds, and the private key allows the spending of these funds through digital signatures. While in theory you could manage your private keys by yourself, in practice it is much more convenient to use a software wallet that will manage your addresses and keys for you, whether that's through a website, directly on your laptop, or on your phone.

One of the most accessible options for first-time users is an **online wallet**. These wallets manage everything on your behalf: they create new addresses each time you need to receive funds (in order to increase your privacy) and create transactions for you when you need to spend your funds. Online wallets are very easy to use and can be a good place for beginners to start. Most exchanges provide free Bitcoin wallets, as do sites such as Blockchain.com.

However, these wallets only provide what is called **hot storage.**[37] They are by nature connected to the internet, and therefore a good target for hackers. As a result, they are not considered very safe and are best used for small amounts only.

To mitigate the risks associated with online wallets, some websites propose optional security through two-factor authentication (2FA). Note that using text messages for 2FA may provide a false sense of security, as text messages can easily be the target of SIM-swapping attacks, where a hacker redirects your phone number to their own phone. In general, it is much safer to use either an "authenticator" app on your phone (this app generates unique codes valid for 30 seconds) or even better, a 2-factor USB key.

Mobile wallets are phone apps that allow users to check their holdings or make payments on the go. They are usually protected by a user-chosen PIN or password. While these mobile wallets are conveniently accessible from your smartphone, they do present some security risks. Not only can your phone be stolen, putting your wallet at risk, but spyware can also be installed, which would compromise the secrecy of the passwords you use. Similarly to online wallets, mobile wallets should only be used for small amounts of cryptocurrencies.

---

[37] The term "hot" refers to something that is online, connected to the internet, and therefore susceptible to hacking.

Online and mobile wallets are great for convenience, in particular for people who intend to spend (or trade) bitcoins regularly. However, if your goal is to invest in bitcoins for the long term (or "HODL" in crypto lingo[38]), or if you are going to store large amounts of cryptocurrencies, even temporarily, you need to use some form of **cold storage.** In other words, you need to store your bitcoins on a device that's not connected to the internet, and hence cannot become a target for hackers.

One of the oldest (and inconvenient) ways to store bitcoins is to use a **paper wallet**. A paper wallet is simply a pair of public and private keys printed on a piece of paper. You can create one using a trustworthy online service such as BitAddress.org (please note that I do not recommend this, especially for large amounts). A small piece of software will run in your computer's browser and use the randomness of your mouse movements and keyboard inputs to generate a pair of public and private keys. The software does not transmit the keys over the internet. All you need to do is print the public and private keys, or even better, write them down.[39] The public key can be used to receive funds, and the private key must be kept in a safe place. (See Figure 45.)

---

[38] The HODL term comes from a 2013 semicoherent internet post by a trader who seemed to be under great stress from not selling at the right time: "I AM HODLING." It has since become Bitcoin lore.

[39] Writing by hand is considered safer, in case there is some kind of spyware infecting your printer.

Figure 45 An example of a paper wallet generated by BitAddress.org. I do not recommend using paper wallets generated this way.

In practice, spending funds from a paper wallet requires using a software wallet as well: when you want to make a payment, you type your address and private keys into the software. Paper wallets can be used—in theory—for long-term storage, but spending only a part of the funds from your paper wallet and leaving the rest is not considered safe: each time you use the private key to make a payment, you risk exposing this private key, for example if your computer has some malware on it.

The main issue with paper wallets is that the algorithms they rely on to create the private keys are usually poorly designed and could potentially lead to several users having the same key, even though *in theory* that is near impossible. That's because the "randomness" they use to create the keys is far from real randomness. This is particularly true of paper wallets created on the internet.

A much better alternative is the use of **hardware wallets**. These are small electronic devices used to generate and store your public and private keys securely while also being able to connect to the internet temporarily so you can spend funds. Even when connected to the internet, hardware wallets do not divulge your private keys; instead, they use them to sign transactions that spend your funds. Only the signatures make it to the internet, not your private keys.

Hardware wallets are considered one of the safest ways to store bitcoins long term while still allowing the user to spend them as needed. These wallets are protected by PINs and/or passwords in a way that makes it very difficult for someone else to access your funds, even if the device is stolen. For example, the delay between two PIN-code attempts is doubled every time an attempt fails, or the device can delete its content after a certain number of failed attempts.

These wallets, as well as most mobile wallets, use a trick that allows them to generate thousands of different addresses and keys from a single secret, called a **seed**. The seed is a list of 12 or 24 words taken from a predefined dictionary of 2,048 words. A new seed is generated the first time you use the wallet. While 24-word seeds provide increased security (just like using a longer password), 12-word seeds are absolutely secure and cannot be cracked with the current technology.

Here's an example of a 12-word seed:

```
ostrich parrot thing dream lab wheat great cattle
nerve thrive waste alpha
```

If you use a hardware wallet, you must keep a copy of your seed in a safe place (or two), as it becomes the only way to recover your funds should the device be lost or stolen, or should you forget your PIN or password[40]. You can also engrave your seed on metal plates sold on the internet (look up

[40] Users locked out of their potential fortunes become the focus of many media stories each time the price of bitcoin soars.

"bitcoin seed plate"). If your hardware wallet gets stolen or lost, you can use your seed to recover your funds and transfer them to a new wallet.

On top of the seed, most hardware wallets can take an extra word or sentence called a passphrase. Each passphrase will generate a unique set of keys, a unique virtual wallet. Even if someone has access to your seed, they would only be able to access an empty wallet. To access your actual wallet, they would also need to know your passphrase. Using a passphrase is highly recommended, but you must make sure that you will not forget your passphrase. Without it, you will have lost all access to your funds, even if you still have your seed!

7.3 Being Your Own Bank: Risks

When you store bitcoins with your own keys (or seed), you inherit most of the security issues that are traditionally associated with banks. You become solely responsible for storing your seeds or private keys securely. The benefit of independence from financial institutions and governments comes at a price: if you lose your private keys or seed words, no one will be able to recover your funds. There is no customer service for Bitcoin!

Therefore, it is essential to store seeds securely and with some redundancy. If you lose your hardware wallet but you still have your seed (and your passphrase), you can recover your funds; you just need to configure a new wallet (software or hardware) with your saved seed. However, if you lose both your seed and your passphrase (for example if your memory is impaired following a road accident), you won't be able to recover your funds.

When it comes to storing bitcoins, here's my advice in a nutshell: use a hardware wallet, use a passphrase, and store copies of your seed in two different locations and a copy of your passphrase in a third location. By doing this you decrease the chance of losing access to your funds while making it difficult for anyone else to access them. This should work very well for any amount between a few hundreds and several thousands of dollars.

However if the amount of cryptocurrency you own is much higher, you may want to implement a more advanced solution, such as a multisignature storage.

7.4 Multisig Storage

As you learned earlier, multisignature addresses (multisigs) are Bitcoin addresses where more than one signature is required to authorize the spending of funds. Multisigs can be used to enhance the security of storing funds.

For example, a 2-of-3 multisig address requires two signatures out of three potential private keys for someone to spend the funds. But the three private keys do not need to belong to different individuals; they can just as well all be yours. Remember that Bitcoin allows you to generate as many private keys and addresses as you want. With such a multisig, you can keep the private keys in three different locations.

Spending funds will require any two signatures. For example, you could keep one private key in your house, another one with an online service, and a third one at your bank or with someone you trust. Neither the online service nor the trusted person can spend your bitcoins on their own.[41] You can access the online service each time you need to spend funds, in conjunction with your own key, thus providing the required two signatures. (See Figure 46.)

---

[41] Unless the online service and the third party collude.

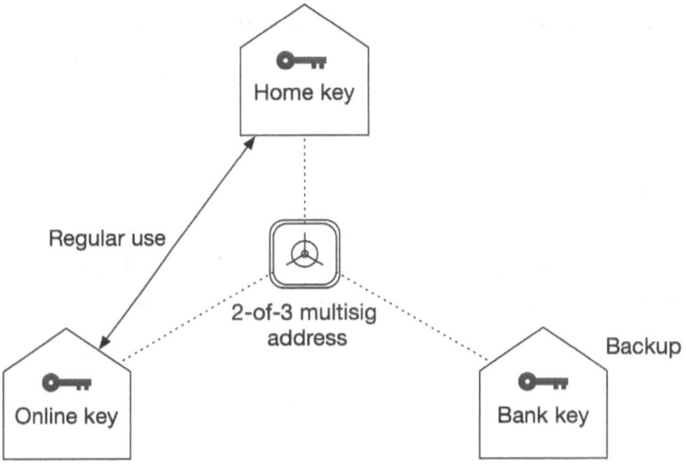

Figure 46 Multisig 2-of-3 storage. The backup key is used only if one of the other two keys is lost or stolen.

If the online service is hacked or corrupted in any way, you can still recover your funds by retrieving the third key from your trusted person. Likewise, if your own key is lost or stolen, not only are your funds safe, but you can access them using the other two keys.

A simple 2-of-3 multisig address can thus greatly improve the security of storing funds by protecting you against theft and loss at the same time. A thief would have to obtain two of your keys to steal your funds, while you can recover your funds even with one key missing. To increase security further, some wallets support up to 5-of-7 multisig addresses, or any other combination that provides safety, recoverability, and ease of use.

Multisig storage is available in some hardware wallets. Setting up a multisig solution is definitely more work than using a simple seed, and how to do it exactly depends a lot on the hardware wallet, but it may be worth it if you need the extra layer of security.

Some protocols are designed for even higher levels of security, say if you need to protect assets worth millions of dollars. The Glacier Protocol, for example, is a very strict, rather complex set of rules that provides extremely high security. The details of such protocols are beyond the scope of this book, just know that they exist.[42]

7.5 Conclusion

Buying and selling bitcoins has become quite simple since 2015, in particular through exchanges. Storing funds safely may appear a bit complicated, depending on the level of security required, but it doesn't need to be. A common strategy is to have different types of wallets for different uses.

For example, you may want to use a hardware wallet to store the larger part of your funds for the long term, but keep smaller amounts in an online or mobile wallet for more regular spending. There are many possibilities for the storage of bitcoins, and no single solution fits all needs. The good news is that as technology evolves and more companies join the cryptocurrency landscape, new solutions that are both secure and practical emerge every day.

Now that you know how Bitcoin works both in theory and in practice, I would like to turn your attention to how it has evolved over time. In the next chapter, you'll learn what changes Bitcoin has gone through and how these changes have been enacted.

---

[42] For example, see GlacierProtocol.org

Chapter 8

Upgrading Bitcoin: Forks Of The Blockchain

8.1 An Evolving Technology

As you now know, the term *bitcoin* refers to several things: the uppercase Bitcoin referring to both the network of computer peers and the software that runs on these nodes, and the lowercase version to the cryptocurrency that this network enables. When we talk about the Bitcoin network, we mean not only the nodes that work within it but also the fact that they all agree on a set of common rules that define valid transactions and blocks. Also known as *consensus rules*, these define how blocks of transitions should look in order to become part of the blockchain.

For example, new bitcoins can only be created as a block reward and not out of thin air. Another example: there is a maximum size allowed for a block. This limitation prevents bottlenecks in the network, among other things.

But having a standard set of rules doesn't mean that the technology is set in stone. On the contrary, Bitcoin has developed continuously since its inception because the rules themselves can evolve. Some rules have remained unchanged (such as the block reward rules[43]), while others have been added, removed, or modified to fix bugs or to make the technology more secure or scalable.

This raises an important question: Who controls the fate of Bitcoin? That is, who decides what, when, and how to upgrade these rules and protocols?

8.2 BIPs: Bitcoin Improvement Proposals

Bitcoin is not a corporate or government entity. There isn't a single person, group, or company making decisions about its evolutions. The cryptocurrency's upgrading paths are open to anyone. Due to the technical nature of Bitcoin, obviously a certain degree of technical knowledge is necessary to propose meaningful changes, but anyone can contribute.

To make a change, formal propositions called **Bitcoin Improvement Proposals**, or BIPs, are collected on a website where the various actors involved in Bitcoin can discuss them. This would include developers, miners, cryptographers, tech companies, and of course regular users.[44]

BIPs are debated publicly until they are either rejected, revised, or accepted. A BIP is accepted when its author has managed to create a general unanimity around it, meaning that there are no significant objections left to the proposal. This is admittedly a rather unclear notion. But the Bitcoin community doesn't like controversial measures; it strives to make everyone happy, which is why changes usually happen quite slowly. The community values the Bitcoin protocol as seriously as Americans view the Constitution: changes must be the exception, not the rule.

---

[43] As a reminder, block reward rules require a fixed maximum supply of 21 million bitcoins.

[44] As of 2020, all the BIPs as well as the source code for Bitcoin's most popular software, Bitcoin Core, were hosted on the website GitHub.com/bitcoin.

Even when a change is adopted by the community, executing it can still be a challenge. It is one thing to update a software application on a laptop, but it is an entirely different affair to update a decentralized network of independent computers, where each person can decide for themselves whether and when to upgrade. So how can this be accomplished without a central authority imposing changes?

8.3 Soft Forks: Backward-Compatible Updates

Even if the Bitcoin community wants to adopt a new set of rules, the nodes can decide individually whether to follow or resist this upgrade. Because Bitcoin is truly decentralized, there is no mechanism to force an individual node, or a group of nodes, to adopt a particular update.[45] That is why the Bitcoin community tries to reach a quasi-unanimous agreement before implementing any upgrade; if most people agree with a change, surely they will implement it too. At least that is the idea.

To make things clearer, let's say that all nodes agree on a set of rules called LEGACY. This simply means that every node runs a software program that follows the rules defined in LEGACY.

The Bitcoin community, or at least a vast majority, would like to upgrade to a new set of rules called NEW. So the community leaders ask all nodes to switch from LEGACY to NEW. It seems easy enough.

But because each node can decide whether to update their software to NEW at the proposed time, do it later, or ignore the update altogether, this creates a considerable risk for Bitcoin. If some nodes use LEGACY rules to check the validity of Bitcoin transactions while other use NEW, the network

45 Other cryptocurrencies have a more centralized decision process. For example, Ethereum is guided by the Ethereum Foundation.

will be split in two parts that don't necessarily recognize each other. As a result, there could be two competing blockchains after the partial upgrade.

Imagine if the government let each person in the US decide whether they want to use Daylight Saving Time or not. That would split the population into two groups that would not even be able to agree on the same time. People would show up at work at different times or miss meetings and appointments, planes would depart without half of their passengers, stock markets would have two different opening times. In other words, it would be pretty chaotic.

In order to avoid such a situation, the Bitcoin community normally updates in a backward-compatible way, so that any block of transactions valid under the NEW rules will also be valid under the LEGACY rules. This way, even if there is a split in the network between nodes who are following the LEGACY rules and those who are following the NEW rules, at least blocks mined according the NEW rules will be accepted by both NEW and LEGACY nodes. In contrast, blocks mined under the LEGACY rules will only be accepted the LEGACY miners. This kind of update is called a **soft fork**, as it doesn't split the network into completely incompatible groups. (See Figure 47.)

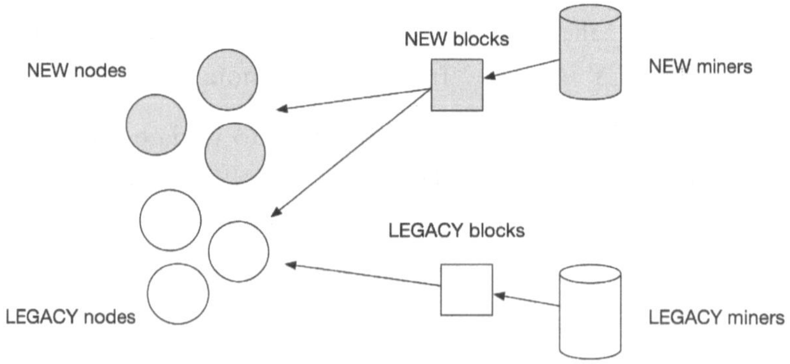

Figure 47 Soft fork, or backward-compatible update: NEW blocks are accepted by everyone.

This is a bit tricky to understand, so let's take some time to analyze what's going on. Consider a set of blocks, some LEGACY and some NEW. The NEW blocks are accepted by all nodes. Most LEGACY blocks will only be accepted by LEGACY nodes; however, some LEGACY nodes will also be compatible with the NEW rules.

So the LEGACY blocks can be split into two groups: the OLD blocks that are incompatible with the NEW rules and the PROGRESSIVE blocks that are compatible with them. (See Figure 48.)

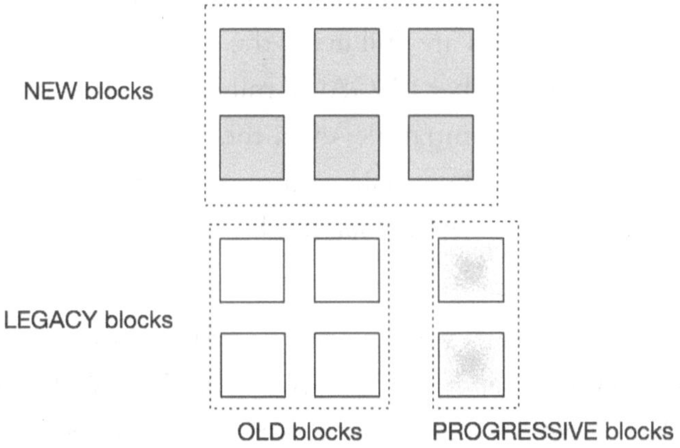

Figure 48 Top: NEW blocks. Bottom: LEGACY blocks split into OLD (incompatible with NEW) and PROGRESSIVE (compatible with NEW).

Imagine that you are a NEW miner, meaning that you have upgraded your software to reflect the new Bitcoin rules. You receive blocks from other miners, either LEGACY or NEW blocks. Obviously, you accept the NEW blocks as valid. As for the LEGACY blocks, you will only accept the PROGRESSIVE blocks, but reject the OLD ones. Thus, the blockchain you construct only contains NEW or PROGRESSIVE blocks.

In particular, if you find a winning block hash and it's your opportunity to add a block to the blockchain, your NEW block will be added on top of a

NEW or PROGRESSIVE block, but it will never be added on top of an OLD block. Figure 49 shows an example.

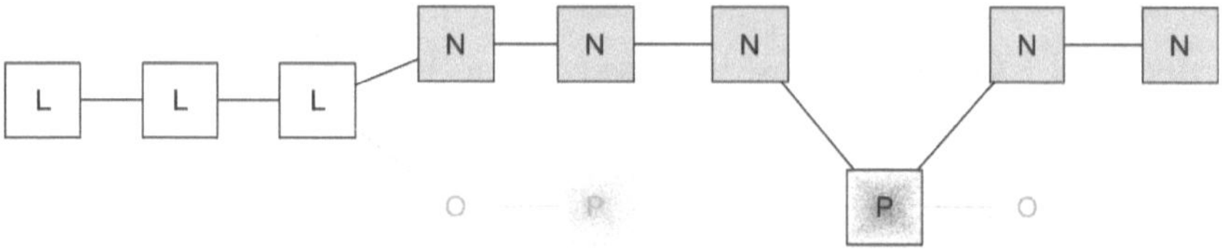

Figure 49 Blockchain seen from a NEW node/miner. The faded blocks are immediately discarded.

Now imagine you are a LEGACY node, which means you haven't upgraded your software and are still using the old Bitcoin rules. You receive new blocks coming from either LEGACY miners or NEW miners. But since the upgrade is backward-compatible, even the NEW blocks are valid under the LEGACY rules, so all the blocks you receive are valid. Your version of the blockchain will thus contain all kinds of blocks: NEW, OLD, and PROGRESSIVE.

Since NEW blocks are never built on top of OLD ones, your blockchain will regularly show ties between OLD blocks and NEW blocks. However, *assuming that NEW miners are a majority* (that is, they have more hashing power than LEGACY miners), the longest chain will always end up being the one that only has NEW or PROGRESSIVE blocks. OLD blocks may show up temporarily, but they will always end up being discarded. (See Figure 50.)

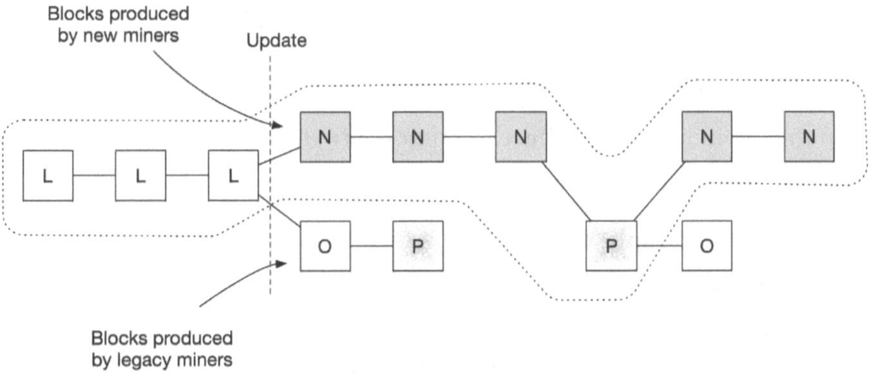

Figure 50 Blockchain seen from a LEGACY node or miner. L = Legacy, O = Old, P = Progressive, N = New. In the end, the longest chain only contains N or P blocks.

In the end, whether you are a NEW or LEGACY node, your version of the blockchain will only contain NEW or PROGRESSIVE blocks. That means miners who produce OLD blocks will never have them permanently in the blockchain, so they will end up wasting time on proof of work and won't be able to cash in on the block rewards.

In other words, miners who have not upgraded will mostly work for nothing. That provides a very strong incentive for ALL miners to upgrade as soon as possible. So although miners cannot be *forced* to upgrade, they can be incentivized to do so.

But what about regular, nonmining nodes? There is no financial incentive for nodes to upgrade, since they do not earn rewards. However, nodes who have not upgraded will not be able to validate the NEW blocks properly; instead, they will validate them using LEGACY rules. Also, it is much easier to update node software than mining software, so there is really not much preventing nodes from updating if they want to keep validating the blockchain properly.

As long as a majority of miners upgrade their software, soon all of them will have done so, and most nodes will probably follow as well. A soft fork is thus the preferred way of upgrading Bitcoin.

You may conclude from this that miners are the ones in charge and nodes just follow, but it would be a simplistic view.

Imagine for example that only a minority of miners want a particular upgrade, but that a majority of regular nodes are in favor of it. If most miners refuse to update their software but most nodes do, then most LEGACY blocks will be rejected by a majority of nodes. In other words, the nodes will tell the miners, "Your blocks are not valid, hence you cannot cash in on your rewards."

Soon enough, the miners will be incentivized to upgrade, even if they didn't want to. As you can see, the balance of power between miners and regular nodes (who outnumber the miners significantly) is a complicated one.

8.4 Some Important Past Forks

Here are some of Bitcoin's most notable soft forks:

- The block size becomes limited to 1 MB in 2010 (done by Nakamoto before BIPs were formalized)
- Pay-to-Script-Hash is added in 2012 (BIP #16)
- The Segregated Witness update increases the actual block size while making transactions more space-efficient in 2017 (BIP #148)

Now, implementing an update as a soft fork is not an easy task. A backward-compatible implementation means that transitions valid under the NEW rules must also be valid under the LEGACY rules. In other words, the NEW rules must be more restrictive. The fact that software can present new features by implementing more restrictive rules seems counterintuitive at first, so let's look at an example.

When you travel abroad, you need a passport. While every country makes its own passports independently, there are some common rules. For example, this document is usually a small booklet with a page dedicated to your photo and identification and several pages dedicated to stamps from your travels.

Now some countries have started to upgrade to biometric passports,[46] which include your biometric data on a small computer chip. A biometric passport, or *e-passport* as it is also called, includes this chip, but also has the traditional pages of a regular passport.

Switching to an e-passport is thus a very typical soft fork: it is more restrictive while implementing new features. It is clearly backward-compatible. A biometric passport can still be used as a regular passport when biometric readers are not available. Therefore, such a transition can happen over time rather than all at once. Individual countries will decide when to upgrade their systems, and citizens will follow slowly as their own passports expire and need to be renewed.

Regular and biometric passports can coexist without causing too much trouble to the system. This is exactly why soft forks are the preferred way to upgrade Bitcoin.

In some cases, however, you need to introduce new features that cannot be implemented in a backward-compatible way. This is true in particular when you want to ease some restrictions: for example if you were to decide that Bitcoin transitions can create more bitcoins than they consume, or that miners can make blocks as large as they want.

---

[46] A biometric passport embeds an electronic chip that contains data used to identify the passport holder, for example by using facial, fingerprint, or iris recognition.

8.5 Hard Forks

While Bitcoin itself is always upgraded through soft forks (at least since 2010), sometimes a fraction of the network wants an upgrade that cannot be backward-compatible. In that case, this group creates a secondary blockchain that will become a competitor of Bitcoin. This is known as a **hard fork**. When this occurs, the blockchain with the most nodes is considered the genuine one (and thus keeps the name Bitcoin), while the least popular blockchain must adopt a new name.

For example, in 2017, a proposal to increase the block size from one megabyte to eight megabytes was only adopted by a minority of Bitcoin miners and nodes. Such an update cannot be done in a backward-compatible way, so the nodes that adopted it hard-forked from the Bitcoin blockchain to create the **Bitcoin Cash** blockchain. In other words, a new cryptocurrency called Bitcoin Cash (or BCH) was created by a minority who disagreed with the legacy rules.

Similarly, a few months after the Bitcoin Cash fork, the Bitcoin Gold blockchain was created by a hard fork from the original Bitcoin blockchain. Bitcoin Gold was intended to restore greater distribution of hash power by preventing the use of specialized hardware by miners. However, this fork also presented some critical drawbacks that failed to convince most Bitcoin nodes. Half a year after the fork occurred, suffering from a rather small following of miners, the Bitcoin Gold blockchain became the target of a successful 51% attack, in which an unknown hacker stole the equivalent of $18 million from an exchange.

Hard forks always split the network—unless they attract 100% of the miners and nodes. While updating 100% of participants is possible for smaller cryptocurrencies or for those where management is less distributed (for example, in Ethereum), it remains impossible for Bitcoin. It is not enough that 100% of miners agree; they must also convince the nonmining nodes. Otherwise, these nodes—who are the validators of the network (and much more numerous than miners)—will reject the new blocks of the update.

For users, a hard fork means that the coins they held in the currency before the fork are now duplicated into coins of the two new currencies. For example, if you held one bitcoin before the 2017 Bitcoin Cash hard fork, afterward you would have held one legacy bitcoin (unchanged) and one Bitcoin Cash (the new currency).

From a financial point of view, a part of the value of Bitcoin was transferred to Bitcoin Cash. Over time, however, the two cryptocurrencies have started to evolve independently.

8.6 Hard Fork Security: Replay Attacks

Hard forks present a particular safety risk: they can be the subject of **replay attacks**. A replay attack exploits the fact that when a hard fork occurs, holdings within the legacy blockchain are duplicated to the newly created blockchain.

Say you found yourself holding one bitcoin (BTC) and one Bitcoin Cash (BCH) just after the hard fork described in the previous section. Then suppose you decide to pay someone one bitcoin. If both blockchains used the same type of addresses and signatures, then an attacker can copy your payment on the bitcoin blockchain and send that copy to the Bitcoin Cash blockchain, triggering a payment that you did not initiate. As a result, you would end up paying not only one BTC but also one BCH. This kind of attack is very unsophisticated but could happen without you even noticing it, if you don't closely monitor your holdings in both cryptocurrencies.

At the same time, replay attacks on cryptocurrencies can be easily prevented. As a user, you can transfer all your new coins to a new address just after the fork. This way, your holdings in the two concurrent blockchains will be associated with different addresses, and a replay attack would fail.

Even better, the developers who proposed the hard fork can include in the new protocol a special marker for all transactions. This way, transactions happening in the old blockchain cannot be replayed in the new one, as they lack the marker. Likewise, transactions in the new blockchain will be considered invalid in the old one because they include a marker that is not recognized.

In practice, all hard forks of cryptocurrencies should include this replay protection. This was the case when Bitcoin Cash was forked from Bitcoin, ensuring that both blockchains were protected from replay attacks after the split.

8.7 Conclusion

In this chapter, you have learned what soft and hard forks are and why Bitcoin prefers to update itself through soft forks: to avoid splitting the network.

In the next chapter, you'll learn about the limitations of Bitcoin in regard to scaling up, which is the ability to be used by millions of users at the same time. Then you will explore how recent developments in Bitcoin technology address these limitations.

Chapter 9

Scaling Bitcoin: Segregated Witness And Lightning Network

9.1 The Scaling Problem

A single Bitcoin transaction takes on average about 500 bytes of space—necessary to describe the inputs, outputs, and signatures/scripts. Each block being limited to 1 MB (or 1 million bytes) can contain around 2,000 transactions.[47] Since the blockchain adds a new block every 10 minutes, this amounts to about three transactions per second: 2,000/(10*60) = 3.33. This is a ridiculously low number for a global payment network.

In comparison, the online payment company PayPal processes around 200 transactions per second, and the card company Visa about 2,000. To put things into perspective, for all human beings on the planet to do just one

[47] This has been slightly increased since July 2017, when the SegWit upgrade was adopted.

transaction per day requires an output of almost 100,000 transactions per second. Bitcoin's three transactions per second was enough during the first years of its existence because very few people knew about it. But as more and more people were willing to transact using this cryptocurrency, it became an issue. Bitcoin just wasn't designed to scale up.

For example, during the peak of the 2017 crypto "bubble," unconfirmed transactions were accumulating in the mempools (the waiting rooms of miners), and it could take hours before any given transaction was mined into the blockchain, instead of the theoretical 10 minutes. And because the mempools were increasing in size, users were willing to pay higher and higher fees to have their transactions jump the queue.

Within a few months, mining fees went from a fraction of a dollar to more than $20 per transaction before going down again when the bubble deflated. This situation highlighted the fact that Bitcoin was not able to compete with other forms of payment for everyday purchases. Why would anyone be willing to pay a $20 fee, or even a $2 fee, each time they bought a coffee, not to mention having to wait 10 or 20 minutes for the payment confirmation? That's pretty expensive for a cup of coffee, especially after it's turned cold. (See Figure 51.)

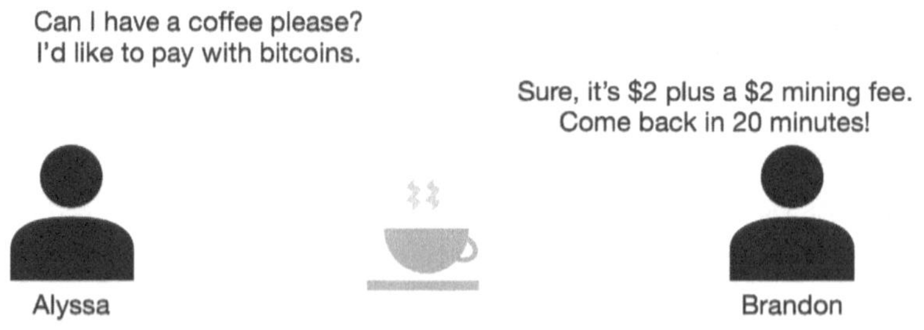

Figure 51 Buying coffee with bitcoins.

There have been two competing models for Bitcoin's use: digital gold (a long-term "store of value") and digital cash (a competitor of fiat money[48] and credit cards). Being a store of value does not necessarily require scaling up. If you own gold, for example, you're probably not going to use it for everyday purchases. Competing with cash and credit cards, however, requires a fast, cheap, and scalable transaction model, which Bitcoin does not have. At least not yet.

Other cryptocurrencies deal with scalability issues using various strategies, and some do achieve much higher throughput than Bitcoin, but not without trade-offs. Scaling up blockchains without compromising decentralization—which is crucial to Bitcoin's independence and security—has proven to be an arduous problem.

9.2 The Block Size Debate

For Bitcoin, there is no simple solution to the scalability issue. One seemingly obvious fix—to increase the block size—became the subject of highly passionate debates in the Bitcoin community in 2017. It might seem like a straightforward solution to the scaling problem, as bigger blocks mined at the same frequency means more transactions per second, but raising the block size would come with several drawbacks.

- It would increase the amount of data circulating on the network and likely create bottlenecks.
- It would make full nodes more expensive to run. Larger blocks would require more hard-drive space to store the blockchain and also more computational power to validate blocks. Therefore the risk of further network centralization would increase, so over time it could become

[48] Fiat money is government-issued currency. For example, the US dollar.

too expensive for individuals to run a full node, leaving this task to corporate entities.

- It would require a hard fork, with a risk of splitting the network.
- Most importantly, no block size increase would be sufficient to reach the throughput necessary to compete with credit card companies, which means that any increase would only be, by nature, a temporary fix.

Because of these drawbacks, there has always been a lot of opposition inside the Bitcoin community to raising the block size. Nevertheless, as mentioned in the previous chapter, in 2017, a minority of nodes and miners decided to increase the block size to eight megabytes, thus forking from Bitcoin to create Bitcoin Cash.

So far, Bitcoin Cash has not been a real success. The number of daily transactions in the Bitcoin Cash blockchain has remained very low, hence the average block size has not been more than 0.2 megabytes, well below the block size limit that motivated the hard fork! Bitcoin Cash itself forked a year later into Bitcoin SV and Bitcoin ABC. (See Figure 52.) Bitcoin ABC is considered the genuine Bitcoin Cash, while Bitcoin SV ("Satoshi's Vision") has been plagued by issues and has been delisted by most exchanges as a result.

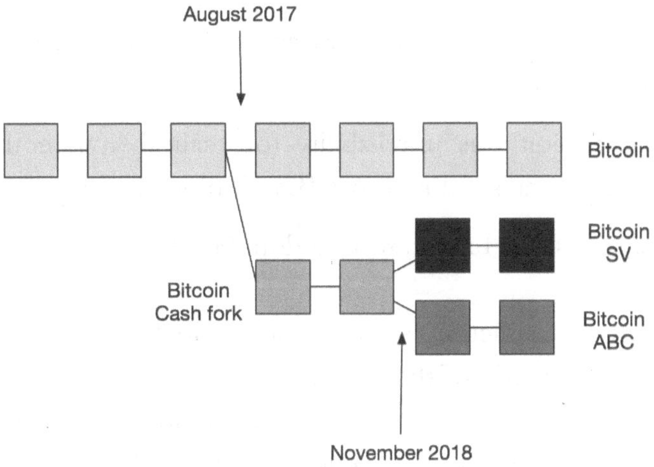

Figure 52 Bitcoin Cash fork and further hard forks.

The alternative to the Bitcoin Cash hard fork was a soft fork called **Segregated Witness**, or SegWit, which would fix a number of flaws in the Bitcoin protocol and lay the ground for further improvements. One of the flaws fixed by SegWit was transaction malleability.

9.3 Transaction Malleability

As you learned, transactions contain inputs and outputs, and each input contains an unlocking script that is usually a signature corresponding to that input. To make transactions easier to process, each one is given a unique number called the *transaction ID* (TXID for short).

The TXID used to be computed in a direct fashion: it was simply the hash of the transaction data. This method was straightforward but presented a weakness: it was easy to slightly alter the unlocking script inside a transaction while keeping the script valid, which resulted in a different hash of the transaction data, and hence a different TXID.[49] In other words, TXIDs were unreliable in the sense that a particular transaction could potentially be found under several TXIDs.

One could exploit this unreliability (or malleability) in the following scenario, where Alyssa is trying to pay Brandon one bitcoin.

1. Alyssa sends one bitcoin to Brandon. Her transaction has a TXID of T1.
2. Before the transaction is mined into a block, Brandon copies it and changes the TXID of that transaction to T2.
3. When the transaction is mined as T2, Brandon has been paid, but he pretends that Alyssa's transaction did not go through.
4. Alyssa checks the blockchain for her transaction T1 and, not seeing it, she assumes the transaction has somehow failed, hence she sends a second payment to Brandon with a TXID of T3.
5. If both T2 and T3 are mined, Brandon will now receive two bitcoins instead of one. See Figure 53.

[49] This could be done for yet unmined transactions (those that are still in the mempool).

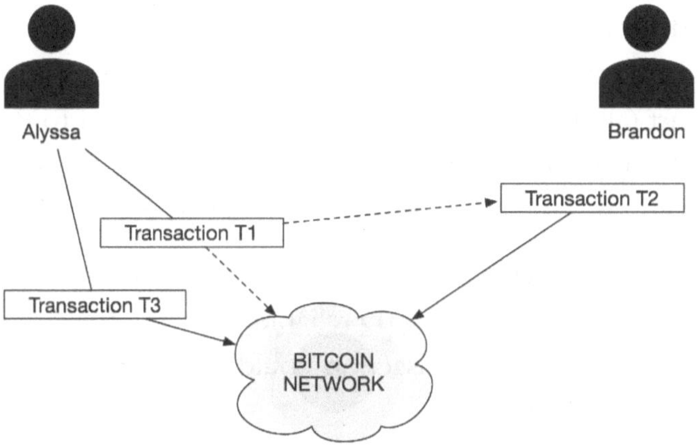

Figure 53 Using malleability, Brandon tricks Alyssa into sending two payments to him instead of one.

The malleability was considered a minor bug at first, as it was fairly easy to protect against fraudulent uses such as the one described above. However, it became a major problem when developers started to look at ways to improve Bitcoin's throughput, as the solution they envisioned relied heavily on unconfirmed transactions, as you will see in the next section.

9.4 Segregated Witness: Making Blocks Bigger Without Saying It

Bitcoin transactions can be fundamentally described as unlocking unspent bitcoins and locking them at new addresses. The signatures, or unlocking scripts, actually account for a lot of the space required to specify the transaction. In other words, unlike signatures on checks in the physical world, digital signatures take quite a bit of room, and room is at a premium in the blockchain.

The key idea behind the 2017 soft fork named Segregated Witness[50] was to split each transaction into its "witness" part (the signatures) and "effective" part (all the rest), and to move the witness part to the end of the transaction. With this new format for transactions, TXIDs were computed in a different way so only the effective part was hashed.

Since only the unlocking script could be modified (now part of the "witness") this little trick made TXID reliable again and fixed the malleability bug for good so that every transaction could only be associated with one TXID. (See Figure 54.)

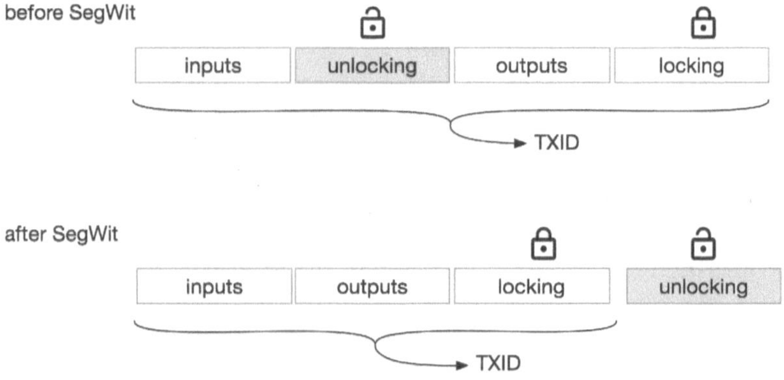

Figure 54 Computing a transaction ID before and after SegWit.

But that's not the only reason to separate the effective and witness parts of each transaction. The SegWit update introduced a new way of counting the space used by the transaction data: effective bytes would weigh the same, but witness bytes would be counted at a 75% discount.

For example, if a transaction were 400 bytes long, with 200 bytes of effective data and 200 bytes of witness data, the new format of the

---

[50] Can you tell this name was chosen by software developers and not by a marketing team?

transaction would make it appear to be only 250 bytes long (200 + 50), a reduction of almost 37%.

Thus, SegWit kills two birds with one stone: it fixes the malleability bug and it makes transactions appear lighter. Of course, this is only an illusion: all the transaction data is still there. But by introducing this new way of counting, the block size could *technically* stay at 1 MB while actually allowing blocks bigger than 1 MB. It's the definition of *size* that has changed.

The reason for using this counting trick is that it allowed the SegWit update to be backward-compatible, and thus to be implemented as a soft fork. Legacy nodes would ignore the new witness format and only count the effective bytes, thus finding the new blocks to still be valid under the old rules.

The bigger blocks allowed by SegWit meant that more transactions could be packed into a single block, hence the transaction throughput could be increased. It could also lead to lower transaction fees: miners could collect more transactions for each block, thus lowering the fee per transaction.

The advantage of proceeding with a soft fork is that legacy and SegWit transactions can cohabit in the blockchain. Backward compatibility ensures that bitcoins can be transferred from old to new addresses and vice versa. SegWit introduced changes while giving users time to adopt them.

Before SegWit, Bitcoin addresses started with "1" or "3." Addresses starting with "1" are the oldest, while addresses starting with "3" were introduced with the Pay-to-Script-Hash soft fork in 2012. SegWit introduced addresses starting with "bc1" (also called *Bech32 addresses*), which presented the following benefits:

- The characters used in Bech32 addresses are always lowercase, making the addresses more comfortable to read out loud or to type on a mobile device (no need to switch between small and large caps)

- Bech32 addresses include a **checksum**, which means that typing errors can be detected with almost 100% certainty; in other words, it becomes almost impossible to send bitcoins to the wrong address because of typing mistakes
- It's faster to generate QR codes from Bech32 addresses than from legacy ones

As of late 2020, three and a half years after the SegWit soft fork, while practically all nodes had updated their software, only about two-thirds of all Bitcoin transactions were using the new format. While updating a node is a relatively straightforward procedure, exchanges and wallet developers have had little incentive to convert entirely to SegWit. It's additional work for them to rewrite their software when they can still use the old format.

As for the actual block size, it has increased by nearly 30% since the soft fork, as lighter transactions slowly replace legacy ones. Segregated Witness has been a success with nodes and miners, and software developers and exchanges are slowly catching up.

This fork may seem like a lot of work for very little progress since the update only allows slightly higher transaction throughputs. But the real strength of SegWit lies elsewhere: by fixing all forms of malleability, it enables second-layer protocols, which are built on top of the Bitcoin one.

9.5 The Lightning Network

The Lightning Network is a protocol first proposed by Joseph Poon and Thaddeus Dryja in 2015 to save space on the blockchain. It works above the blockchain, on top of the Bitcoin protocol, and therefore is called a **second-layer protocol**.

What do I mean by "above the blockchain"? Having all transactions recorded in the blockchain is slow, uses space, encumbers the network, and takes up computer time for all network nodes. To free space on the blockchain, second-layer protocols allow individuals to do most of their transactions "off-chain," while only using the blockchain to record landmark transactions.

Let's look at an example to clarify. Every morning Alyssa goes to the same coffee shop, owned by Ben, to get her caffeine fix. It would be absurd for Alyssa to pay Ben with bitcoins using regular, on-chain transactions.

- For one thing, the transaction fees would add significantly to the price of her coffee
- Also, Ben would have to wait every morning for Alyssa's payment to be mined in the blockchain to make sure it went through

Instead, Alyssa and Ben decide to open a "tab," similar to a bar tab. Every time Alyssa orders coffee, the price would be added to the tab and, at some point, she would need to settle the total. Of course, Ben would need to trust that Alyssa was not going to drink coffee for a month, then disappear without paying her tab.

The Lightning Network enables Alyssa and Ben to create a digital tab using bitcoins. Such a tab is called a **channel**. Alyssa funds the channel by sending one bitcoin (to simplify) to a multisig address that is locked by hers and Ben's signatures (both need to agree in order to spend these locked funds). This is called a **commitment transaction**: Alyssa has committed one bitcoin to her coffee habit at Ben's, but she is putting this money in a box that requires both signatures in order to be opened.

However, Alyssa doesn't want Ben to take off with that box. Even though he can't open it by himself, her money would still be missing. So before sending the commitment transaction to the Bitcoin network, she asks Ben to sign a refund from that multisig address, just in case he decides to disappear. This refund is a payment from the commitment box back to Alyssa. Thus, even if Ben were to take off (or just stop cooperating), she could sign the refund (she already has his signature on it) and get her money back.

Once Alyssa has received the refund, she keeps it for herself and sends the commitment transaction to the Bitcoin network, making the commitment effective. Now Alyssa and Ben are ready to do business. (See Figure 55.)

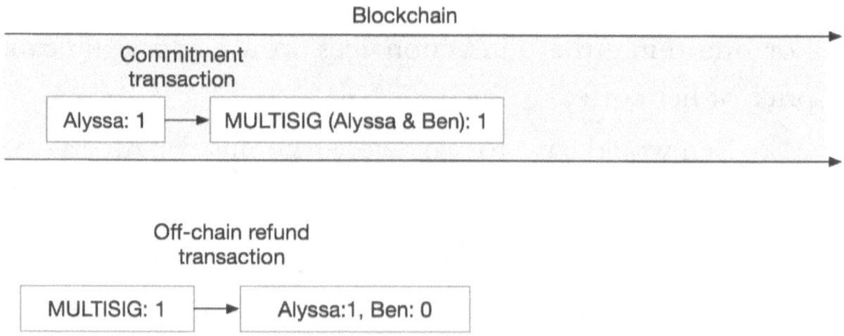

Figure 55 Opening the tab: Alyssa commits one bitcoin to a new channel with Ben, but keeps the refund off-chain.

Each time Alyssa goes to Ben's coffee shop, the commitment box's balance is modified to reflect the new payment. Let's say a coffee costs 0.001 bitcoins.

1. The first time Alyssa orders, she signs a transaction from the commitment box paying 0.001 bitcoins to Ben and the remainder (0.999 bitcoins) to herself.
2. She sends that transaction to him.
3. Upon receipt, Ben sends a signed copy back to Alyssa.
   This is like an IOU, but better: even if Alyssa disappears, Ben can retrieve the funds transferred to him. No need to go to court to settle it or pay attorneys; simply broadcasting the latest transaction to the network will make the payment happen. But for now, Ben can hold on to the IOU without sending it to the network, as he expects Alyssa to come back soon for another coffee.

4. The next time Alyssa buys coffee from Ben, she updates the IOU. She sends Ben a new transaction using funds from the commitment box, but this time paying him 0.002 bitcoins (she's had two coffees so far) and the rest (0.998 bitcoins) to herself.
   This IOU is more advantageous to Ben than the previous one, so he can toss the old one. Again, in case Alyssa decides to stop cooperating, he can sign the latest IOU received and recover his part of the funds. (See Figure 56.)

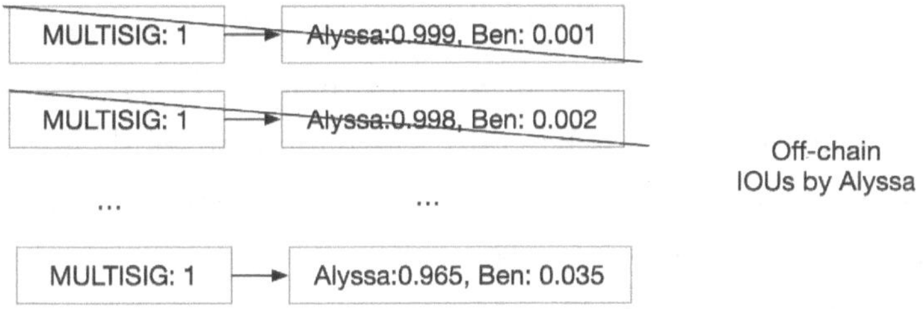

Figure 56 Off-chain IOUs: only the latest one is valid.

Now, what happens if it's Ben who stops cooperating? Alyssa is still protected because he cannot spend more than the amount that appeared in the most recent IOU, since the multisig requires both signatures to unlock the funds.

Without needing to trust each other, Alyssa and Ben can keep doing business this way, completely out of sight of the Bitcoin network. At any time either Ben or Alyssa can decide to close the channel by broadcasting the latest IOU to the network: that is called the **settlement transaction**. (See Figure 57.)

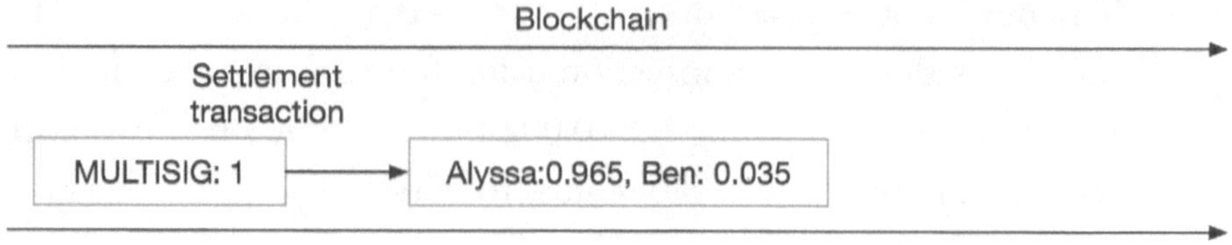

Figure 57 Closing the tab: the settlement transaction is mined into the blockchain.

There is no need to send all the daily exchanges that have happened in between. Only the commitment transaction and the settlement transaction must be mined into the blockchain. All the rest happened off-chain, and therefore without having to wait for confirmations or to pay any mining fees. All these daily transactions have been instantaneous and almost free.[51] Even if Alyssa has paid Ben 500 times using the Lightning Network, only two transactions will be written into the blockchain. That's obviously a phenomenal gain of space.

The only risk for Ben is that Alyssa could be tempted to cheat by sending the initial refund to the blockchain rather than her most recent IOU. To ensure that she is not able to use a refund other than the latest one, a combination of mechanisms is built into the Lightning Network that severely punishes any participant who tries to cheat. This is done by a combination of **time locks** (so that some parts of the refund cannot be cashed out immediately) and secret keys.

If Alyssa tries to cheat Ben by broadcasting any payment other than the latest one, the time locks give Ben enough time to counteract and get back the funds before Alyssa takes them.

---

[51] The use of the Lightning Network is not completely free, but the fees are minuscule compared the mining fees of the base layer.

In practice, the Lightning Network does even better than managing digital tabs: both participants can commit funds to the channel in the commitment transaction, allowing payment channels to work both ways.

Furthermore, the Lightning Network does not always require Alyssa and Ben to open a payment channel directly; instead, they could use already opened channels through common intermediaries. For example, if Alyssa had an open channel with Charlie, Charlie had one with Dee, and Dee had one with Ben, then Alyssa and Ben could start doing business immediately without opening a new channel, further alleviating the load on the blockchain.

Why was SegWit necessary to implement the Lightning Network? Because by using the malleability bug, Alyssa and Ben could have altered some payment IDs, and that would have made the guarantees provided much more challenging to structure.

9.6 The Future Of The Lightning Network

The Lightning Network is still in its infancy, and it is not a miracle solution to Bitcoin's scaling problem…not yet anyway. In theory, it enables a much higher number of transactions per second than the blockchain: a channel can allow thousands of transactions to happen *off-chain* while requiring only two *on-chain* transactions. By enabling quasi-instant and quasi-free transactions at a very large scale, the Lightning Network would also open the door to digital micropayments, which were not possible before because of transaction fees—for example, payments by the second for streaming music and movies.

The Lightning Network is not devoid of problems, however. One of them is that it can currently only be used for small payments (a few dollars). Another is that the funds committed to the opening of a channel are frozen until that channel is closed, thus limiting the number of channels a user will be willing to open. Finally, at this stage, the Lightning Network is still a very experimental technology and thus is not 100% reliable. It is still rather complex to use, although this is changing rapidly, in particular thanks to new digital wallets and apps. It is too early to say if this is indeed the ideal scaling solution for Bitcoin, but it is undoubtedly a promising piece of the puzzle.

Chapter 10

Limitations And Opportunities

Bitcoin's future is still highly unpredictable. However, what we can do is look at the main limitations of the cryptocurrency and see what roads can be taken to overcome them. In this final chapter, I'll address several arguments that critics have raised regarding Bitcoin, and discuss their validity.

10.1 Is Bitcoin Too Centralized?

Bitcoin's philosophy[52] relies on these core principles:

- Open: Anyone can inspect the Bitcoin code, and anyone can read the blockchain and participate in the network
- Neutral: Bitcoin doesn't favor anyone nor does it follow any particular nation's rules

---

[52] At least, this is the philosophy defended by a large part of the Bitcoin community.

- Secure: Nodes don't need to trust each other to keep the network safe and operational[53]
- Decentralized: The system is spread among many nodes, preventing any particular person, company, or government from taking over

In the first few years (2009–2010), Bitcoin mining could be done on regular computers using standard CPUs (central processing units, the main chips of computers). But as more and more people joined the network, the **difficulty** increased, requiring more computing power to mine successfully.

Mining bitcoins began to require more and more computing power. So GPUs (graphics processing units), which are very good at parallel tasks, replaced CPUs for a time, only to be replaced by ASICs around 2013.

Since ASICs—which are quite expensive to buy and consume a lot of electricity—have taken over the Bitcoin mining network, mining has become a big-money industry. You can still mine bitcoins on your computer at home, but your odds of finding a block before anyone else is almost null. In response, mining pools have appeared, where individuals can join forces (computational resources) to increase their chances of finding a block at the cost of dividing the profit between pool members.

Bitcoin mining has become mostly a corporate venture that locks in significant capital and uses tons of energy. Since 2013, China has been both a great purveyor of cheap electricity and home to the main ASIC manufacturers. As a result, an important share of Bitcoin's hashrate (the total computing power devoted to mining) is done on Chinese land.

---

[53] On the internet, this is often referred to as Bitcoin being "trustless."

This is problematic for Bitcoin, as ultimately its security relies on the difficulty of executing a 51% attack. Having a significant share of the hashrate located in China puts the network at risk.

For example, the government could coerce the mining farms into wreaking havoc on the network by accepting a "double-spend," which would severely undermine Bitcoin's public image. Doing so would be very costly and counterproductive from an economic standpoint. However, it could still be done for political reasons, for instance to get rid of Bitcoin by destroying the public's trust in its independence and resistance to censorship. While it is true that the rest of the network, after a double-spend attack, could decide to "fork" away from the Chinese blockchain, it would probably be challenging to gain back the lost confidence.

Notably, since 2018, the trend of miners being concentrated in China has actually reversed a little, and mining has become more geographically diverse again. However, as long as China provides cheap energy and Bitcoin relies on the proof-of-work algorithm, the geographic concentration of miners remains a valid concern.

10.2 Is Bitcoin Destroying The Planet?

Proof of work, the algorithm at the heart of Bitcoin mining, is energy-voracious: it consumes a lot of power to produce little. In fact, it is designed to be wasteful. Every 10 minutes, only one hash calculation is written into the blockchain, even though the network has been working at roughly 100 exahashes[54] per second in the meantime. And only one out of these 6×10^{22} calculations is used by the blockchain! All the energy used by the other calculations is "wasted," in the sense that it is not used for any other purpose.

---

[54] An exahash is 10^{18} hashes.

Of course, this is an oversimplistic view. In reality, this wastefulness is what secures the network; it is the mechanism through which the decentralized "lottery ticket" is drawn. And more power, more energy used for mining means more security for Bitcoin. The cost of attacking the network is proportional to the global energy used by all miners. With the present electrical power dedicated to Bitcoin mining, it has become impossibly costly for a single country to take over the network and perform such an attack. However, as noted previously, that doesn't mean there are no risks at all.

Proof of work performs well because it encourages both energy consumption and investment in hardware. Both factors contribute to the network's security. There are actual, and extremely high, costs to attacking Bitcoin. Someone would need the physical assets (the ASICs) and the energy associated with their operation.

But since the difficulty keeps going up in proportion to the increase of hashing power, mining has indeed become an arms race. Every few months, a new and more efficient ASIC chip is produced and sold to miners looking for an edge in the race. As a result, Bitcoin's hashrate has gone from one exahash per second (2016) to 10 exahashes (2017) to 100 exahashes (2019). At the end of 2020, the hashrate stood at about 130 exahashes per second.

Proof of work is not the only algorithm available to cryptocurrencies. Alternatives, such as proof of stake, are increasingly being used in order to prevent the wastefulness associated with proof of work. Some cryptocurrencies, for example Ethereum, are even trying to transition fully from proof of work to proof of stake.

In proof of work, miners participate by dedicating their time and energy to computing hashes. In proof of stake, miners (called **validators**) do not solve a mathematical problem; instead, they deposit some amount of cryptocurrency as stake and get selected randomly to validate the next block. The bigger the stake, the more likely a validator is to be selected.

A selected validator will be able to collect all transaction fees from the block but does not get any other reward. If a validator is selected and tries to put a fraudulent transaction into the block, the network will take away a portion of its stake. This discourages fraudulent behavior. A majority attack is still possible but is very costly, as an attacker must deposit a higher stake than the rest of the network combined.

The staking mechanism is also supposed to encourage decentralization, as validators don't need to group into pools, in opposition to proof of work. The main drawback of proof of stake lies in the positive feedback loop it creates: wealthy validators are able to stake more funds, get more chances of winning the next block and its transaction fees, and hence end up having even more funds to stake for the next round.

Several mechanisms can be attached to the selection process in order to make proof of stake more fair, for example taking the stake's "age" into account (as in how long the funds have been staked). However, the long-term implications of proof of stake are not yet fully understood and might be a cause for concern. In this regard, it will be fascinating to see what happens when the Ethereum network actually switches fully to proof of stake.

The bottom line is that while proof of stake is extremely energy efficient and thus more ecological than proof of work, it hasn't yet been shown to be completely safe or fair in the long term.

10.3 Is Bitcoin Too Transparent?

Bitcoin is pseudo-anonymous by design; funds are allocated to addresses, not to names. While this provides some level of privacy, it is not very difficult to de-anonymize some addresses.

Cryptocurrency exchanges usually have strict KYC rules in order to discourage money laundering and tax evasion. To enforce these rules, customers have to provide some kind of identification. Exchanges then make assumptions regarding addresses that their customers use to send or receive funds.

If, for instance, you send the totality of the funds held on an exchange to an external address (such as a hardware wallet), the exchange can assume that you are the owner of that external address too. If, from this external address, you split your funds into equal parts to different new addresses right after receiving them, the odds that you are also the owner of these new addresses are again quite high. And so on.

Blockchain analysis companies use sophisticated heuristics [55] to de-anonymize transactions. Exchanges hire these companies to protect themselves legally from any money laundering activity, drug-related funds, and more. For example, they can decide to ban a user based on the probability that their funds come from a dark market[56] or have been used for online gambling.

Privacy is not a concern limited to those who conduct illegal activities. The transparency of Bitcoin's blockchain means that anyone who knows one

---

55 Heuristics are rules based on probabilities.

56 Dark markets are illegal markets based on the dark net, the "invisible" part of the internet.

of your addresses also knows all the transactions that have gone through that address.

Imagine if all your bank statements were published on the internet. That wouldn't be a pleasant experience, even if you had nothing to hide. Bitcoin has no built-in feature to protect its users from such disclosure. The only measure you can take is preventive: never use the same address twice to receive payments, in order to make it more difficult for third parties to de-anonymize your addresses.

But privacy has long been on the mind of Bitcoin developers. In recent years, an exciting scheme known as *Schnorr signatures* has been developed, which significantly increases privacy while also improving efficiency in the blockchain.

When bitcoins move from one address to another, digital signatures are used to unlock these funds. Bitcoin currently uses ECDSA signatures. They work well and are quite secure, and the algorithm they use is open source, meaning that it is not subject to any copyright. However, ECDSA signatures take quite a bit of space (a problem that is only partially addressed by SegWit), and a signature is required for each input of a transaction. So a transaction with five inputs typically has five signatures.

Schnorr signatures take less space than ECDSA signatures, but most importantly, the former ones can be aggregated. Signature aggregation means that different signatures can be added together, and the result will be a valid signature. In the previous example, instead of all five signatures being written into the transaction, they can be combined into a single signature, and the unique result will be valid for all five of the inputs. That means a lot of space can be saved in the blockchain.

Imagine that Alyssa, Ben, Dee, and Elena have all sent bitcoins to a multisig address that requires any two of them to sign. If Alyssa and Dee collaborate to spend the bitcoins stored at this address, their public keys and their signatures will have to appear in the transaction they're sending to the blockchain. Therefore, everyone will know that it's them, and not Ben and Elena, spending these bitcoins.

With Schnorr signatures, however, Alyssa's and Dee's signatures can be aggregated into a single one, and this alone is enough to spend the bitcoins but not enough to reveal who the two signees are. Even when this transaction is published in the blockchain, no one will know exactly who—between Alyssa, Ben, Dee, and Elena—authorized the spending. As a result, all participants benefit from increased privacy.

Schnorr signatures also make it impossible to distinguish between a regular transaction and a multisignature transaction because they look exactly the same. Once again, that makes it harder to de-anonymize transactions.

And finally, Schnorr signatures encourage the use of CoinJoin, a scheme where multiple users combine their individual transactions into a common one in order to hinder the de-anonymization analysis.

Schnorr signatures have already been integrated, as of May 2019, by Bitcoin's rival Bitcoin Cash (but through a mandatory hard fork). It will probably take a little more time to implement them in Bitcoin, but it seems like these signatures are definitely in the cryptocurrency's future.[57]

---

[57] Schnorr signatures were proposed in BIP 340.

Chapter 11

Conclusion

Let's summarize what you have learned regarding Bitcoin:

- The Bitcoin network is an open and decentralized structure made up of nodes and miners. The miners bundle transactions into blocks and compete to add their block to the blockchain by trying to solve proof-of-work puzzles. The nodes make sure that the miners follow the rules.
- Coins are held at addresses, which are generated from private keys. The safety of these keys is the cornerstone of Bitcoin's security.
- Transactions (payments) have inputs and outputs. Inputs use digital signatures to validate the authenticity of the senders. Outputs use addresses to specify where the funds go. Addresses are pseudonymous, but transactions are completely public.
- New bitcoins are only created in the first transaction of any block, and the amount created by each block is cut in half roughly every four years. This reward is collected by the miner who solves the proof-of-work puzzle first, along with fees from all the transactions in the block.

- Bitcoin solves ties between miners by using the "longest-chain" rule. This rule can in theory be exploited to launch attacks, but the combined power of Bitcoin's miners makes such an attack too expensive to be realistic.
- Bitcoin provides additional mechanisms such as multisignature addresses and scripting, which allows for more complex scenarios.
- Changes to the protocol happen by a consensus of the majority. Soft forks, or backward-compatible updates, are the preferred way to upgrade Bitcoin. Sometimes minorities split away from Bitcoin by a hard fork to create a new cryptocurrency.
- Bitcoin's blockchain is slow, adding only around 2,000 transactions every 10 minutes on average, but recent updates have allowed second-layer protocols to be developed, potentially increasing that speed by several orders of magnitude.
- While Bitcoin still relies on energy-hungry proof of work, there are alternative algorithms, such as proof of stake, which would not consume so many resources.
- Finally, privacy is also on the mind of Bitcoin developers, and some improvements are to be expected in the coming years.

As you can see, Bitcoin has strengths and weaknesses. Besides, thousands of other cryptocurrencies have been created since 2009, and while most will probably go extinct, some will certainly endure. Understanding Bitcoin will make it much easier for you to sort through this jungle of new cryptocurrencies and assess which ones bring something valuable to users and which don't. In any case, Bitcoin has a special place in this ecosystem: it retains a first-mover advantage and is still the dominant force due to the size of its network.

Finally, Bitcoin is also a social experiment. Can we trust a form of money that is not backed by any government? Is Bitcoin digital cash or digital gold?

Maybe Bitcoin will be used only as a store of value while a different cryptocurrency will be used for daily transactions. Or maybe Bitcoin itself will fall into oblivion and a new cryptocurrency will replace it completely.

I have no doubt, however, that the future is bright for cryptocurrencies in general. These new digital currencies are not going away; on the contrary, they keep gathering more interest from governments, corporations, investors, and regular users alike.

So, where can you go from here? Here's, to conclude, a list of actions you can take that will help you further your understanding:

- Buy a small amount of bitcoin on a well-known crypto-exchange (as of writing: Kraken, Gemini, Coinbase, Coinmama…). You don't have to buy a whole bitcoin, it can be as small a fraction as you want.
- Set up a crypto-wallet app on your smart phone (as of writing: Blockstream Green, Coinnomi, or Zengo for example are available for both iOS and Android devices.)
- If you have more than a few hundred dollars of Bitcoin, buy a hardware wallet and send your funds there (as of writing: Ledger and Trezor are both easy to use but new brands are coming up.)
- Send a payment to yourself or to someone else. See if you can choose the fee or if the wallet is setting it automatically. See how long it takes for the payment to be confirmed.
- Find that transaction on a block explorer (for example: blockchain.org or blockstream.info.)
- Ask questions on internet forums (such as BitcoinBeginners on Reddit) but never reveal your identity or the amount of your holdings.

- Download a wallet that allows you to do payments on the Lightning Network (as of writing: Wallet of Satoshi, Breez, or Éclair.)
- And if you want to dive deeper, run a full node yourself by installing BitcoinCore on your computer (bitcoincore.org.)

I hope that this book has convinced you that Bitcoin is anything but a scam, even though it may attract scammers (like most things that are internet-based.) That it is not a perfect technology, but a perfectible one. And that, even though you already know a lot about Bitcoin, there is always more to learn.

In the following pages you will find a glossary, references, and a short list of online resources. Thank you for reading this book. I wish you the best on your journey into cryptocurrencies.

Glossary

(cryptocurrency) exchange: Virtual marketplace for buyers and sellers of cryptocurrencies. Examples in the US include: Coinbase, Gemini, and Kraken.

51% attack: An attack on any cryptocurrency that attempts to rewrite its blockchain by taking over the majority (51% or more) of the mining nodes. See also *majority attack*.

address: A string of letters and numbers used to identify where someone stores their bitcoins, similar to a postal address or a PO Box. Example: `bc1qxy2kgdygjrsqtzq2n0yrf2493p83kkfjhx0wlh`.

ASIC (application-specific integrated circuit): Computer chip designed for a very specific task. In the Bitcoin context, they are designed to find proof-of-work solutions. Modern ASICs can perform several trillions of operations per second. Their performance is measured in terahashes per second. The most popular ASIC miners are Bitmain's Antminer series (China).

Bitcoin Cash: Cryptocurrency rival of Bitcoin, created by a hard fork in 2017. Allows the block size to go up to 8 MB, compared to Bitcoin's 1 MB. Symbol: BCH.

Bitcoin Gold: Cryptocurrency rival of Bitcoin, created by a hard fork in 2017. Uses the Equihash algorithm for mining instead of Bitcoin's proof of work. Was the subject of successful majority attacks in 2018 and 2020. Symbol: BTG.

Bitcoin Improvement Proposal (BIP): A formal proposal to improve or fix features of the Bitcoin protocol and code. BIPs are gathered on the website github.com/bitcoin, where they are debated by the community of Bitcoin developers and other actors. Example: BIP-42 fixed a bug in the Bitcoin code that would have let the supply of bitcoins grow indefinitely.

Bitcoin protocol: A set of common rules that defines how bitcoins are created, how transactions are validated, and how blocks are formed. Also called *consensus rules*. Example: a transaction cannot create more bitcoins than it consumes, except for a coinbase transaction.

Bitcoin: The cryptocurrency invented by Satoshi Nakamoto in 2008 based on a peer-to-peer network using a distributed ledger and cryptographic proof of work. Symbol: BTC.

block: A batch of transactions bundled together by miners. Each block is limited to 1 MB in size since 2010 and a little more since the SegWit update in 2017. A block is added to the blockchain every 10 minutes on average, regardless of the number of miners and their total computing power.

blockchain: A chain of blocks linked in chronological order and secured by cryptography. Bitcoin's blockchain adds a new block of transactions every 10 minutes on average. As of 2020, the size of the blockchain was over 300 GB (gigabytes).

BTC: Abbreviation/symbol for Bitcoin.

channel: A communication link between two users of the Lightning Network so they can exchange payments instantly without using the blockchain.

coinbase transaction: First transaction of every block, where the miner collects the block reward and transaction fees. Coinbase transactions allow the creation of new bitcoins, thus increasing Bitcoin's monetary supply.

cold storage: Type of Bitcoin wallet usually not connected to the internet, and thus less subject to hacking. Examples: hardware wallets or paper wallets.

commitment transaction: Opening transaction in a Lightning Network channel that allows participants to commit funds to their future payments.

confirmations: Number of blocks since a transaction has been recorded in the blockchain. The more confirmations a transaction receives, the more irreversible it becomes. One confirmation means the transaction is in the latest block.

consensus rules: Set of rules that governs Bitcoin (See **Bitcoin protocol**); common state of the blockchain agreed on by most miners.

difficulty: Factor that determines how many guesses miners need on average to find a valid proof-of-work solution. The difficulty adjusts automatically every 2,016 blocks: if more miners join the network, the difficulty goes up, and conversely if miners leave.

digital signature: Cryptographic data that can be computed from a private key and is used to authenticate the sender of a transaction. Bitcoin uses

ECSDA signatures, which are impossible to forge in the current state of technology.

double-spending: Attempting to spend a digital token or coin twice. To avoid double-spending, all coins must be tracked. In Bitcoin, this is done by recording every transaction in the blockchain.

ECDSA (Elliptic Curve Digital Signature Algorithm): Cryptographic algorithm used by Bitcoin to generate signatures from private keys and therefore ensure that bitcoins can be spent by their rightful owners and no one else.

exahash per second: Unit used to measure the mining power dedicated to Bitcoin around the world. 1 exahash / second = 10^{18} hashes / second. (See **hashrate**.)

fee: Part of a payment that goes to miners. Transaction fees reward miners for participating in the network. The higher the fee, the quicker miners will pick up the transaction and add it to the blockchain. Fees are usually expressed in satoshis/bytes.

fork: A permanent split, change, or update of the blockchain. See also *hard fork* and *soft fork*.

full node: A participant (node) of the network that validates every transaction received in every block. Full nodes check that miners behave honestly, but unlike miners, they do not receive any payment for this work.

hard fork: A split of the blockchain into two incompatible branches. A hard fork can also designate a new cryptocurrency created by such a split. Example: Bitcoin Cash is a hard fork from Bitcoin.

hardware wallet: An electronic device that manages all aspects of securely receiving and sending bitcoins.

hash or **hashing:** A mathematical function that assigns a unique output of fixed length to any input such that one cannot reconstruct the input from the output. Also called a *one-way function.* Example: SHA-256 is a hash function used in Bitcoin that computes a 256-bit output for an input of any size.

hashrate: Total number of computations per second that the miners are currently completing. Gives a measure of the global computing power dedicated to mining. Usually expressed in exahashes per second (10^{18} hashes computations per second). Example: Bitcoin's hashrate was around 130 exahashes at the end of 2020.

hot storage: Bitcoin wallet usually connected to the internet, which thus can become the target of hackers. Example: an online wallet.

input: Part of a transaction that specifies which coins are being transferred.

key: Piece of information used to either locate funds in the blockchain (See **public key**) or spend funds (See **private key**).

Know Your Customer (KYC): Set of laws that is meant to prevent money laundering activities by linking financial accounts to customer identities.

ledger: Another name for the blockchain; records all Bitcoin transactions.

Lightning Network: A second-layer protocol that enables instant and almost free transactions between parties without accessing the blockchain frequently.

longest-chain rule: Allows Bitcoin nodes to decide between competitive version of the blockchain. The longest chain, the one with the most blocks, is the one kept.

majority attack: An attack on any cryptocurrency that attempts to rewrite its blockchain by taking over the majority of the mining nodes. See also *51% attack.*

mempool: Set of transactions received by the Bitcoin network but not yet written into the blockchain. The mempool contains unconfirmed transactions.

Merkle root: Hash of all the transactions in a block, when they are arranged in a data structure resembling a tree, which is also known as a *Merkle tree.*

miner: Participant (node) of the Bitcoin network who dedicates computing power and electricity to finding proof-of-work solutions and eventually writes new transactions into the blockchain. Miners compete with each other, and the winner receives the block reward and transaction fees associated with the winning block.

multisig: Multisignature address; a special type of address that requires several signatures to release the funds it stores. Example: a 2-of-3 multisig requires two signatures from any of the three participants.

node: A participant in Bitcoin's peer-to-peer network. Regular nodes validate the work of miners by checking that new blocks conform to the consensus rules.

nonce: An integer that miners change many times per second when they are searching for a proof-of-work solution to a new block. Each new value of the nonce gives a new chance to find a solution.

output: Part of a transaction that specifies to which addresses bitcoins are being transferred and under which conditions they can be spent.

paper wallet: A type of Bitcoin wallet where the private key is simply written down and hidden until it is needed. Paper wallets are only safe if they are generated from perfectly random numbers. They are very impractical.

Pay-to-public-key (P2PK): Simplest script used to lock some funds to someone's public key. P2PK is considered obsolete and has been replaced by P2PKS.

Pay-to-public-key-script (P2PKS): Script that locks funds to someone's public key, but without showing the public key itself and instead using the hash of that key. It has become a replacement for the obsolete P2PK. The public key is only revealed when the spending occurs.

Pay-to-script-hash (P2SH): Script that locks funds to the hash of any script, allowing for example the creation of multisig addresses or more complex scenarios. The script itself is not made public until the funds have to be spent.

peer-to-peer: A network of computers where each participant, called a *peer*, communicates with a limited number of neighbors. A peer-to-peer network does not have a precise structure and does not need a centralized control.

private key: A string of letters and numbers that can unlock funds at a corresponding Bitcoin address. A private key is like a combination to a safe.

proof of stake: Alternative algorithm to proof of work that uses very few computing resources and therefore can be implemented without wasting energy. Proof of stake is more recent than proof of work and is still considered controversial by many.

proof of work: Algorithm used by Bitcoin to secure the blockchain by intentionally wasting energy and computing power, therefore making it costly to change the content of any block.

pseudonymous: Mode of operation where users are identified by a pseudonym rather than their actual names. In Bitcoin, these pseudonyms are the addresses.

public key: A string of letters and numbers that can be computed from a private key and distributed safely to others without compromising the private key. The public key can be used to compute the address.

Satoshi Nakamoto: The pseudonymous creator of Bitcoin and author of the Bitcoin whitepaper (2008). Satoshi was an active participant in a cryptography mailing list but ceased all communications in December 2010.

satoshi: A very small sub-unit of bitcoin. One bitcoin is worth 100 million satoshis. The satoshi is the smallest unit permitted by the blockchain.

Schnorr signature: A signature scheme meant to replace the ECSDA signatures of Bitcoin by improving privacy.

script: Limited computing language used in Bitcoin to check that signatures are valid, and to create other conditions. Scripting is the basis of smart contracts.

second-layer protocols: Protocols designed to allow communications in a peer-to-peer network while only accessing the first layer, the blockchain, very occasionally. Example: the Lightning Network.

Segregated Witness (SegWit): A soft fork update adopted by the majority of Bitcoin nodes and miners in the summer of 2017. It allows for blocks slightly larger than 1 MB, fixed several issues, and created a new category of addresses called *Bech32*.

settlement transaction: Opening contract of a Lightning Network channel where participants commit funds to their future payments.

SHA-256: The most used hash function in Bitcoin. As of 2020, it was considered extremely secure because it is practically impossible to reverse.

smart contract: Set of conditions expressed in computer language (script) that defines when and how a transaction is supposed to be executed. Ethereum, a rival of Bitcoin, made smart contracts the focus of its features.

soft fork: An update of a cryptocurrency that can be adopted by miners and nodes over time. Example: SegWit was a soft fork update adopted in summer 2017 by the Bitcoin network.

target: Factor that determines how many guesses miners need on average to find a valid proof-of-work solution. The lower the target, the more guesses on average. The target is adjusted every 2,016 transactions (around two weeks) to keep the average time between blocks at 10 minutes.

time lock: A condition that can restrict the spending of some bitcoins until a specified time in the future. It is written using Bitcoin Script code.

transaction: A Bitcoin payment; takes inputs (previously unspent coins) and outputs (where the coins are transferred to and under which conditions they can be spent); usually includes a fee that is collected by the first miner to write that transaction into the blockchain.

UTXO (unspent transaction output): A coin that has not been spent yet. Each miner maintains a database of UTXOs so they can check that new transactions only spend valid coins.

validation: The action of checking that a transaction or a block of transactions adheres to the Bitcoin rules.

validators: In proof of stake, miners are replaced with validators.

wallet: A collection of addresses and private keys that can be managed by software, by hardware, or by an app on a mobile device.

References

"A complete history of Bitcoin's consensus forks." BitMEX.com. December 28, 2017. https://blog.bitmex.com/bitcoins-consensus-forks/.

Agrawal, Harsh. "What is Bitcoin Cash (BCH) – Everything You Need To Know." CoinSutra.com. August 12, 2019. https://coinsutra.com/bitcoin-cash-bch/.

Antonopoulos, Andreas. *Mastering Bitcoin: Programming the Open Blockchain.* O'Reilly Media. 2004.

Beigel, Ofir. "A Beginner's Guide to Bitcoin Paper Wallets." 99Bitcoins.com. Last updated October 23, 2020. https://99bitcoins.com/bitcoin-wallet/paper/.

Bitcoin ATM Map search. CoinATMRadar.com. https://coinatmradar.com.

Bitcoin Avg. Transaction Fee historical chart. BitInfoCharts.com. https://bitinfocharts.com/comparison/bitcoin-transactionfees.html.

"Bitcoin Difficulty Chart." CoinWarz.com. https://www.coinwarz.com/mining/bitcoin/difficulty-chart.

Bitcoin SegWit Adoption. Woobull.com. https://charts.woobull.com/bitcoin-segwit-adoption/.

Bitcoin/BTC Price. CoinDesk.com. https://www.coindesk.com/price/bitcoin.

Boyd, Andrew. "Comparing Fingerprints." University of Houston. The Engines of our Ingenuity, No. 2529. UH.edu. https://www.uh.edu/engines/epi2529.htm.

"Caesar Cipher." McGill School of Computer Science. 2007. https://www.cs.mcgill.ca/~rwest/wikispeedia/wpcd/wp/c/Caesar_cipher.htm.

"Can Blockchain Bank the Unbanked?" AiThority.com. February 4, 2020. https://aithority.com/technology/blockchain/can-blockchain-bank-the-unbanked/.

Chen, James. "Liberty Reserve." Investopedia.com. Updated September 26, 2020. https://www.investopedia.com/terms/l/liberty-reserve.asp.

Christine, Kim. "The Rise of ASICs: A Step-by-Step History of Bitcoin Mining." CoinDesk.com. April 27, 2020. https://www.coindesk.com/rise-of-asics-bitcoin-mining-history.

"Confederate Cipher Disc." CryptoMuseum.com. https://www.cryptomuseum.com/crypto/usa/ccd/index.htm.

Conway, Luke. "Bitcoin halving." Investopedia.com. Updated May 11, 2020. https://www.investopedia.com/bitcoin-halving-4843769.

CryptoQuant Team. "Introduction to Bitcoin Heuristics." CryptoQuant.com. July 30, 2019. https://medium.com/cryptoquant/introduction-to-bitcoin-heuristics-487c298fb95b.

Curran, Brian. "What Are Replay Attacks in Cryptocurrency? Complete Beginner's Guide." Blockonomi.com. June 27, 2018. https://blockonomi.com/replay-attacks/.

Dheivanai. "Localbitcoins Vs Paxful – A Detailed Comparison." Bitdeal.net. December 19, 2020. https://www.bitdeal.net/localbitcoins-vs-paxful.

Dowling, Stephen. "Napster turns 20: How it changed the music industry." BBC.com. May 31, 2019. https://www.bbc.com/culture/article/20190531-napster-turns-20-how-it-changed-the-music-industry.

Download Bitcoin Core. BitcoinCore.org. 2020. https://bitcoincore.org/en/download/.

Editors of *Encyclopedia Britannica.* "Yap Islands." Britannica.com. https://www.britannica.com/place/Yap-Islands.

"e-Passports." US Department of Homeland Security. DHS.gov. https://www.dhs.gov/e-passports.

Ethereum.org. www.ethereum.org.

"FAQs: Currency Redesign." US Department of the Treasury. Bureau of Engraving and Printing. MoneyFactory.gov. https://www.moneyfactory.gov/resources/faqs.html.

"Fingerprints." CrimeMuseum.org. https://www.crimemuseum.org/crime-library/forensic-investigation/fingerprints/.

Frankenfield, Jake. "HODL." Investopedia.com. Updated June 30, 2020. https://www.investopedia.com/terms/h/hodl.asp.

Frankenfield, Jake. "Satoshi." Investopedia.com. Updated June 27, 2020. https://www.investopedia.com/terms/s/satoshi.asp.

"Glacier Protocol." Glacierprotocol.org.

Gladstone, Rick. "How Venezuela Fell Into Crisis, and What Could Happen Next." NYTimes.com. May 27, 2016. https://www.nytimes.com/2016/05/28/world/americas/venezuela-crisis-what-next.html.

Global Bitcoin Nodes Distribution. Bitnodes.io. 2021. https://bitnodes.io.

Gross, Grant. "Debate over encryption access isn't going away." WashingtonExaminer.com. January 9, 2020. https://www.washingtonexaminer.com/policy/technology/debate-over-access-to-encryption-isnt-going-away.

Hertig, Alyssa. "Bitcoin Gold Initiates Hard Fork Split to Create New Cryptocurrency." CoinDesk.com. October 24, 2017. https://www.coindesk.com/bitcoin-gold-initiates-hard-fork-split-create-new-blockchain.

"Hexadecimal Definition." The Linux Information Project. Linfo.org. http://www.linfo.org/hexadecimal.html.

"History of QR Code." QRCode.com. https://www.qrcode.com/en/history/.

"History of the Enigma." CryptoMuseum.com. https://www.cryptomuseum.com/crypto/enigma/hist.htm.

Kenton, Will. "CoinJoin." Investopedia.com. Updated December 5, 2020. https://www.investopedia.com/terms/c/coinjoin.asp.

Kissi, Dawn. "Venezuela is trying to float its own cryptocurrency to save a sinking economy—but investors aren't believing the 'petro' hype." CNBC.com. January 21, 2018. https://www.cnbc.com/2018/01/19/venezeulas-petro-currency-met-with-skepticism-by-investors.html.

Leiner, Barry M., Vinton G. Cerf, David D. Clark, Robert E. Kahn, Leonard Kleinrock, Daniel C. "Liberty Reserve digital cash chief jailed for 20 years." BBC.com. May 9, 2016. https://www.bbc.com/news/technology-36247289.

"Lightning: Victim Data." US Centers for Disease Control and Prevention. CDC.gov. Last reviewed December 23, 2013. https://www.cdc.gov/disasters/lightning/victimdata.html.

Lynch, Jon Postel, Larry G. Roberts, Stephen Wolff. "Brief History of the Internet." InternetSociety.org. 1997. https://www.internetsociety.org/internet/history-internet/brief-history-internet/.

Leyden, John. "Mafia boss undone by clumsy crypto." TheRegister.com. April 19, 2006. https://www.theregister.com/2006/04/19/mafia_don_clueless_crypto/.

"Mempool Size (Bytes)." Blockchain.com. https://www.blockchain.com/charts/mempool-size.

Mishra, Deepak. "Understanding bitcoin transaction fee per byte." Metamug.com. May 11, 2020. https://metamug.com/article/security/bitcoin-transaction-fee-satoshi-per-byte.html.

Motluk, Alison. "Fingerprints may illuminate life in the womb." NewScientist.com. November 30, 2005. https://www.newscientist.com/article/dn8396-fingerprints-may-illuminate-life-in-the-womb/.

Muzzy, Everett. "What Is Proof of Stake?" ConsenSys.net. May 15, 2020. https://consensys.net/blog/blockchain-explained/what-is-proof-of-stake/.

Nakamoto, Satoshi. "Bitcoin: A Peer-to-Peer Electronic Cash System." PDF. Bitcoin.org. https://bitcoin.org/bitcoin.pdf.

Nimfuehr, Marcell. "The Amazing Story of Cryptocurrencies Before Bitcoin." HackerNoon.com. November 5, 2018. https://hackernoon.com/the-amazing-story-of-cryptocurrencies-before-bitcoin-fe1b0e55155b.

Noll, Franklin. "Lincoln's Greenback Mill: Civil War Financing and the Start of the Bureau of Engraving and Printing, 1861–1863." Society for History in the Federal Government. Federal History. 2009. http://shfg.org/resources/Documents/FH%201%20(2009)%20Noll.pdf.

Ogundeji, Olusegun. "Antonopoulos: Your Keys, Your Bitcoin. Not Your Keys, Not Your Bitcoin." Cointelegraph.com. August 10, 2016. https://cointelegraph.com/news/antonopoulos-your-keys-your-bitcoin-not-your-keys-not-your-bitcoin.

Phillips, Daniel. "Why is Bitcoin's supply limit set to 21 million?" Decrypt.co. December 30, 2020. https://decrypt.co/34876/why-is-bitcoins-supply-limit-set-to-21-million.

"PIN." Trezor wiki. https://wiki.trezor.io/PIN.

Poon, Joseph and Thaddeus Dryja. "The Bitcoin Lightning Network: Scalable Off-Chain Instant Payments." January 14, 2016. https://lightning.network/lightning-network-paper.pdf.

"QR Code Generator." https://www.qr-code-generator.com/solutions/bitcoin-qr-code/.

"Quantitative Easing (QE)." Investopedia.com. Updated January 3, 2021. https://www.investopedia.com/terms/q/quantitative-easing.asp.

RaspberryPi.org. https://www.raspberrypi.org.

Redman, Jamie. "Bitcoin Cash Protocol Successfully Upgrades—Schnorr Signatures Are Here." Bitcoin.com. May 15, 2019. https://news.bitcoin.com/bitcoin-cash-protocol-successfully-upgrades-schnorr-signatures-are-here/.

Richard. "TXID (Transaction Identifier) Explained." Mycryptopedia.com. October 29, 2018. https://www.mycryptopedia.com/txid-transaction-identifier-explained/.

Roberts, Jeff John. "Bitcoin Spinoff Hacked in Rare '51% attack'." Fortune.com. May 29, 2018. https://fortune.com/2018/05/29/bitcoin-gold-hack/.

Ross, Sean. "Understanding How the Federal Reserve Creates Money." Investopedia.com. Updated September 22, 2020. https://www.investopedia.com/articles/investing/081415/understanding-how-federal-reserve-creates-money.asp.

Salter, Philip. "China's leadership in the Bitcoin mining industry will be challenged." Cointelegraph.com. November 14, 2020. https://cointelegraph.com/news/china-s-leadership-in-the-bitcoin-mining-industry-will-be-challenged.

Sharma, Rakesh. "Bitcoin Gold Hack Shows 51% Attack Is Real." Investopedia.com. Updated May 30, 2018. https://www.investopedia.com/news/bitcoin-gold-hack-shows-51-attack-real/.

Tharngan, John. "Stone Money." The Road to Riches, programme 2. BBC.co.uk. http://news.bbc.co.uk/hi/english/static/road_to_riches/prog2/tharngan.stm.

"The birth of the Web." CERN. https://home.cern/science/computing/birth-web.

"Total Hash Rate." Blockchain.com. https://www.blockchain.com/charts/hash-rate.

"USA PATRIOT Act." Financial Crimes Enforcement Network. FinCen.gov. https://www.fincen.gov/resources/statutes-regulations/usa-patriot-act.

Walters, Steve. "Best Bitcoin Multisignature Wallets: Top 7 Places to Hold BTC." CoinBureau.com. June 19, 2019. https://www.coinbureau.com/analysis/bitcoin-multisignature-wallets/.

BitcoinWiki (BitcoinWiki.org)

"Bitcoin address." Last modified on March 18, 2019. https://en.bitcoinwiki.org/wiki/Bitcoin_address.

"Bitcoin Improvement Proposals." Last modified on March 25, 2019. https://en.bitcoinwiki.org/wiki/Bitcoin_Improvement_Proposals.

"Elliptic Curve Digital Signature Algorithm." Last modified on March 31, 2019. https://en.bitcoinwiki.org/wiki/Elliptic_Curve_Digital_Signature_Algorithm.

"Private key." Last modified on February 9, 2020. https://en.bitcoinwiki.org/wiki/Private_key.

"SHA-256." Last modified on April 29, 2019. https://en.bitcoinwiki.org/wiki/SHA-256.

Bitcoin Wiki (BitcoinWiki.it)

"BIP 0173." Last modified September 24, 2019. https://en.bitcoin.it/wiki/BIP_0173.

"Genesis block." Last modified July 13, 2020. https://en.bitcoin.it/wiki/Genesis_block.

"Invoice address." Last modified October 23, 2020. https://en.bitcoin.it/wiki/Invoice_address.

"Laszlo Hanyecz." Last modified May 7, 2017. https://en.bitcoin.it/wiki/Laszlo_Hanyecz.

"Multisignature." Last modified November 25, 2019. https://en.bitcoin.it/wiki/Multisignature.

"Pay to script hash." Last modified December 30, 2017. https://en.bitcoin.it/wiki/Pay_to_script_hash.

"Principles of Bitcoin." Last modified September 17, 2017. https://en.bitcoin.it/wiki/Principles_of_Bitcoin.

"Protocol documentation." Last modified December 14, 2020. https://en.bitcoin.it/wiki/Protocol_documentation.

"Satoshi (unit)." Last modified February 15, 2018. https://en.bitcoin.it/wiki/Satoshi_(unit).

"Scalability." Last modified December 29, 2020. https://en.bitcoin.it/wiki/Scalability.

"Schnorr." Last modified May 25, 2020. https://en.bitcoin.it/wiki/Schnorr.

"Transaction." Last modified December 13, 2019. https://en.bitcoin.it/wiki/Transaction.

Online Resources

www.bitcoin.org is the official website of the Bitcoin community, with great resources for all practical and theoretical aspects of the cryptocurrency.

www.investopedia.com has excellent short explanations for all concepts related to Bitcoin, cryptocurrencies, and investing.

www.blockexplorer.com is a straightforward blockchain explorer where you can investigate blocks, transactions, inputs, and outputs.

www.fermatslibrary.com/s/bitcoin has an annotated version of the original 2008 white paper by Satoshi Nakamoto, "Bitcoin: A Peer-to-Peer Electronic Cash System."

www.reddit.com/r/BitcoinBeginners/ is an active online community for new users of Bitcoin where they can ask questions.

www.reddit.com/r/Bitcoin/ is an online community dedicated to "Bitcoin: The Currency of the Internet" and also to memes, especially during high volatility.

Made in United States
Troutdale, OR
11/03/2026

56847378R00096